POST STITCH

Work around post of stitch indicated, inserting hook in direction of arrow **(Fig. 4)**.

Fig. 4

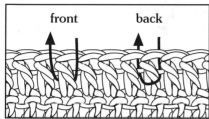

front   back

WHIPSTITCH

Place two pieces with **wrong** sides together. Sew through both pieces once to secure the beginning of the seam, leaving an ample yarn end to weave in later. Working through **both** loops on **both** pieces **(Fig. 5a)** or through **inside** loop of each stitch on **both** pieces **(Fig. 5b)**, ★ insert the needle from front to back through next stitch and pull yarn through; repeat from ★ across.

Fig. 5a

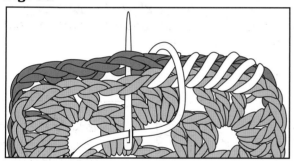

Fig. 5b

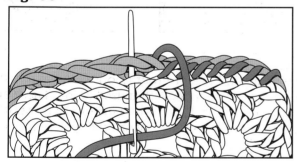

FRINGE

Cut a piece of card[board] fringe specified in in[structions]. **loosely** and **evenl**[y] until the card is fille[d] needed.

Hold together as many strands of yarn as specified in individual instructions; fold in half.

With **wrong** side facing and using a crochet hook, draw the folded end up through a row, stitch, or space and pull the loose ends through the folded end **(Fig. 6a or 6c)**; draw the knot up **tightly** **(Fig. 6b or 6d)**. Repeat, spacing as specified in individual instructions.

Lay flat on a hard surface and trim the ends.

Fig. 6a

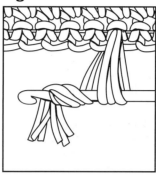

Fig. 6b

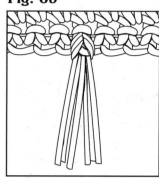

Fig. 6c

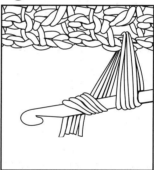

Fig. 6d

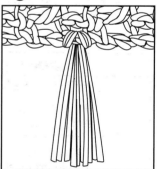

# All American

Finished Size: 45" x 70"

MATERIALS
Worsted Weight Yarn:
  Ecru - 18 ounces, (510 grams, 1,135 yards)
  Red - 17 ounces, (480 grams, 1,070 yards)
  Blue - 8 ounces, (230 grams, 505 yards)
Crochet hook, size J (6.00 mm) **or** size needed
  for gauge
Yarn needle

GAUGE: In pattern, (3 dc, ch 1) 4 times = 4¼";
          7 rows = 4"

Gauge Swatch: 4" straight edge to straight edge
Work same as Motif.

STITCH GUIDE

TREBLE CROCHET *(abbreviated tr)*
YO twice, insert hook in st or sp indicated, YO and
pull up a loop (4 loops on hook), (YO and draw
through 2 loops on hook) 3 times.

RIGHT DECREASE *(uses next 2 dc)*
YO twice, insert hook in next dc, YO and pull up a
loop, (YO and draw through 2 loops on hook) twice,
YO, insert hook in next dc, YO and pull up a loop,
YO and draw through 2 loops on hook, YO and draw
through all 3 loops on hook.

LEFT DECREASE *(uses next 2 dc)*
YO, insert hook in next dc, YO and pull up a loop,
YO and draw through 2 loops on hook, YO twice,
insert hook in next dc, YO and pull up a loop, (YO
and draw through 2 loops on hook) twice, YO and
draw through all 3 loops on hook.

CLUSTER *(uses next 2 sps and next joining)*
† YO 3 times, insert hook in **next** sp, YO and pull
up a loop, (YO and draw through 2 loops on hook) 3
times †, YO 3 times, insert hook in next joining, YO
and pull up a loop, (YO and draw through 2 loops on
hook) 3 times, repeat from † to † once, YO and draw
through all 4 loops on hook.

STAR FIELD
MOTIF (Make 46)
With Ecru, ch 3; join with slip st to form a ring.

Rnd 1 (Right side)**:** Ch 1, 12 sc in ring; join with slip st
to first sc.

Note: Loop a short piece of yarn around any stitch to
mark Rnd 1 as **right** side.

Rnd 2: Ch 2, (YO, insert hook in **next** sc, YO and
pull up a loop, YO and draw through 2 loops on hook)
twice, YO and draw through all 3 loops on hook, ★ ch 4,
YO, insert hook in **same** sc, YO and pull up a loop, YO
and draw through 2 loops on hook, (YO, insert hook in
next sc, YO and pull up a loop, YO and draw through
2 loops on hook) twice, YO and draw through all 4 loops
on hook; repeat from ★ 4 times **more** working last st in
same sc as beginning ch-2, ch 4; join with slip st to top
of first st, finish off: 6 ch-4 sps.

Rnd 3: With **right** side facing, join Blue with slip st in
any ch-4 sp; ch 1, 6 sc in same sp and in each ch-4 sp
around; join with slip st to first sc: 36 sc.

Rnd 4: Ch 3 **(counts as first dc, now and
throughout)**, dc in next 2 sc, ch 2, (dc in next 6 sc,
ch 2) 5 times, dc in last 3 sc; join with slip st to first dc,
finish off: 36 dc and 6 ch-2 sps.

HALF MOTIF (Make 6)
Row 1 (Right side)**:** With Blue, ch 4, 8 dc in fourth ch
from hook **(3 skipped chs count as first dc)**: 9 dc.

Note: Mark Row 1 as **right** side.

Row 2: Ch 1, turn; sc in first dc, (2 sc in next dc, sc in
next dc) across: 13 sc.

Row 3: Ch 3, turn; dc in same st and in next sc, 2 dc
in next sc, dc in next sc, ★ (dc, ch 2, dc) in next sc, dc
in next sc, 2 dc in next sc, dc in next sc; repeat from ★
once **more**, (dc, ch 3, slip st) in last sc; finish off: 20 sts
and 2 ch-2 sps.

ASSEMBLY
With Blue, working through **both** loops, and using
Placement Diagram as a guide, page 4, whipstitch
Motifs and Half Motifs together forming 4 vertical strips
of 7 Motifs **and** 3 vertical strips of 6 Motifs and 2 Half
Motifs *(Fig. 5a, page 2)*, beginning in second ch of first
corner ch-2 and ending in first ch of next corner ch-2;
then whipstitch strips together in same manner.

PLACEMENT DIAGRAM

Point A

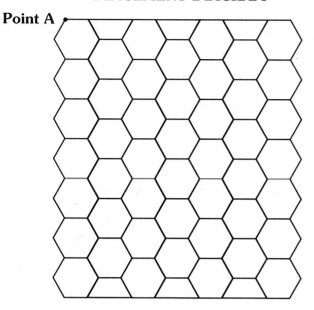

EDGING

With **right** side facing, join Blue with slip st in ch-2 sp at Point A; † ch 4, tr in next dc, work right decrease, dc in next dc, hdc in next 2 dc, sc in next ch-2 sp, hdc in next 2 dc, dc in next dc, work left decrease, ★ tr in next dc, work Cluster, tr in next dc, work right decrease, dc in next dc, hdc in next 2 dc, sc in next ch-2 sp, hdc in next 2 dc, dc in next dc, work left decrease; repeat from ★ 5 times **more**, tr in next dc and in next ch-2 sp, 3 sc around tr just made, sc in same sp as tr, sc in next 6 dc and in next sp; (working in end of rows on Half Motif, 2 sc in first row, sc in next row, 2 sc in next row, sc in ch at base of 9-dc group, 2 sc in next row, sc in next row, 2 sc in next row, sc in next sp, sc in next 6 dc and in next sp) 3 times †, slip st in same sp, repeat from † to † once, 3 sc around beginning ch-4; join with slip st to top of beginning ch-4, finish off.

STRIPES

With Red, ch 265 **loosely**.

Row 1 (Right side)**:** Dc in fourth ch from hook **(3 skipped chs count as first dc)** and in next ch, ★ ch 1, skip next ch, dc in next 3 chs; repeat from ★ across: 66 3-dc groups.

Note: Mark Row 1 as **right** side.

Row 2: Ch 5 **(counts as first dc plus ch 2, now and throughout)**, turn; 3 dc in next ch-1 sp, (ch 1, 3 dc in next ch-1 sp) across, ch 2, skip next 2 dc, dc in last dc: 65 3-dc groups.

Row 3: Ch 3, turn; 2 dc in next ch-2 sp, (ch 1, 3 dc in next ch-1 sp) across to last ch-2 sp, ch 1, 2 dc in last sp, dc in last dc: 66 3-dc groups.

Row 4: Ch 5, turn; 3 dc in next ch-1 sp, (ch 1, 3 dc in next ch-1 sp) across, ch 2, skip next 2 dc, dc in last dc: 65 3-dc groups.

Rows 5 and 6: Repeat Rows 3 and 4 changing to Ecru at end of Row 6 *(Fig. 2a, page 1)*.

Rows 7-12: Repeat Rows 3 and 4, 3 times changing to Red at end of Row 12.

Rows 13-18: Repeat Rows 3 and 4, 3 times changing to Ecru at end of Row 18.

Rows 19-36: Repeat Rows 7-18 once, then repeat Rows 7-12 once **more**.

Row 37: Ch 3, turn; 2 dc in next ch-2 sp, (ch 1, 3 dc in next ch-1 sp) 39 times, leave remaining sts unworked: 40 3-dc groups.

Rows 38-42: Repeat Rows 2-6: 39 3-dc groups.

Rows 43-78: Repeat Rows 7-18, 3 times; at end of Row 78, do **not** change colors and do **not** finish off.

EDGING

Ch 1, turn; with corresponding color, sc evenly around entire piece working 3 sc in each corner and decreasing at inner corner; join with slip st to first sc, finish off.

With Blue, whipstitch Star Field into upper left hand corner of Stripes.

Design by Linda Luder.

4

Bold Beauty

Finished Size: 49" x 65"

MATERIALS
Worsted Weight Brushed Mohair Blend:
   Purple - 14 ounces, (400 grams, 1,240 yards)
Worsted Weight Yarn:
   Teal - 32 ounces, (910 grams, 2,150 yards)
   Navy - 4 ounces, (110 grams, 270 yards)
Crochet hooks, sizes J (6.00 mm) **and** N (9.00 mm)
   or sizes needed for gauge

GAUGE: In pattern, with small size hook,
         13 dc and 7 rows = 4"
         In pattern, with large size hook,
         13 hdc and 8 rows = 4"

Gauge Swatches: 4" square
With Teal and small size hook, ch 15 **loosely**.
Row 1: Dc in fourth ch from hook **(3 skipped chs count as first dc)** and in each ch across: 13 dc.
Rows 2-7: Ch 3 **(counts as first dc)**, turn; dc in next dc and in each dc across.
Finish off.

With Purple and large size hook, ch 14 **loosely**.
Row 1: Hdc in third ch from hook **(2 skipped chs count as first hdc)** and in each ch across: 13 hdc.
Rows 2-8: Ch 2 **(counts as first hdc)**, turn; hdc in next hdc and in each hdc across.
Finish off.

Note: Each row is worked across length of Afghan.

STITCH GUIDE

TREBLE CROCHET *(abbreviated tr)*
YO twice, insert hook in st indicated, YO and pull up a loop (4 loops on hook), (YO and draw through 2 loops on hook) 3 times.

SLANT STITCH *(abbreviated Slant St)*
   (uses next 4 sts)
Skip next 3 sts, tr in next st, working **behind** tr just made, dc in 3 skipped sts.

AFGHAN BODY
With Purple and large size hook, ch 213 **loosely**.

Row 1: Hdc in third ch from hook **(2 skipped chs count as first hdc)** and in each ch across: 212 hdc.

Row 2 (Right side)**:** Ch 3 **(counts as first dc, now and throughout)**, turn; working in Back Loops Only *(Fig. 1, page 1)*, dc in next hdc, work Slant Sts across to last 2 hdc, dc in last 2 hdc: 52 Slant Sts.

Note: Loop a short piece of yarn around last dc made to mark Row 2 as **right** side and bottom edge.

Row 3: Ch 2 **(counts as first hdc, now and throughout)**, turn; hdc in Front Loop Only of next st and each st across: 212 hdc.

Row 4: Ch 3, turn; working in Back Loops Only, dc in next st, work Slant Sts across to last 2 sts, dc in last 2 sts: 52 Slant Sts.

Row 5: Ch 2, turn; hdc in Front Loop Only of next st and each st across: 212 hdc.

Rows 6-16: Repeat Rows 4 and 5, 5 times; then repeat Row 4 once **more** changing to Teal at end of Row 16 *(Fig. 2a, page 1)*.

Row 17: With small size hook, ch 3, turn; dc in Front Loop Only of next st and each st across.

Row 18: Ch 3, turn; dc in Back Loop Only of next st and each st across.

Row 19: Ch 3, turn; dc in both loops of next dc and each dc across.

Rows 20-24: Repeat Rows 18 and 19 twice, then repeat Row 18 once **more** changing to Purple at end of Row 24.

Row 25: With large size hook, ch 2, turn; hdc in both loops of next dc and each dc across.

Rows 26-33: Repeat Rows 4 and 5, 4 times changing to Teal at end of Row 33.

Rows 34-39: With small size hook, repeat Rows 18 and 19, 3 times changing to Purple at end of Row 39.

Rows 40-43: With large size hook, repeat Rows 4 and 5 twice changing to Teal at end of Row 43.

Rows 44-48: With small size hook, repeat Rows 18 and 19 twice, then repeat Row 18 once **more** changing to Purple at end of Row 48.

Row 49: With large size hook, ch 2, turn; hdc in both loops of next dc and each dc across.

Rows 50 and 51: Repeat Rows 4 and 5 changing to Teal at end of Row 51.

Rows 52-54: With small size hook, repeat Rows 18 and 19 once, then repeat Row 18 once **more** changing to Purple at end of Row 54.

Rows 55-61: Repeat Rows 49-54 once, then repeat Row 49 once **more**.

Row 62: Repeat Row 4 changing to Teal in last dc.

Rows 63 and 64: Repeat Rows 17 and 18; at end of Row 64, finish off.

Row 65: With **right** side facing, large size hook, and working in both loops, join Purple with slip st in first dc; ch 3, dc in next dc, work Slant Sts across to last 2 dc, dc in last 2 dc changing to Teal in last dc.

Row 66: Repeat Row 17; finish off.

Row 67: With **wrong** side facing, large size hook, and working in both loops, join Purple with slip st in first dc; ch 2, hdc in next dc and in each dc across changing to Teal in last hdc.

Rows 68-94: With small size hook, repeat Rows 18 and 19, 13 times; then repeat Row 18 once **more**.

Finish off.

FIRST STRIPE

Row 1: With **right** side facing, large size hook, working from bottom to top on Row 17, and holding Navy at back, insert hook from **front** to **back** in sp **between** first and second dc, YO and pull up a loop, ★ skip next sp, insert hook in next sp, YO and **loosely** draw through sp and loop on hook; repeat from ★ across to last dc, slip st around post of last dc.

Row 2: Ch 1, **turn**; slip st **loosely** in each slip st across inserting hook from top to bottom; finish off.

ADDITIONAL STRIPES

Work same as First Stripe on Rows 34, 44, 52, 58, 63, 66, and 68.

Using photo as a guide, page 30, and holding either 6 strands of Purple yarn, 6 strands of Teal yarn, **or** 3 strands of Navy yarn together, each 19" long, add fringe in end of rows across short edges of Afghan **(Figs. 6c & d, page 2)**.

Design by Rena Stevens.

Classic Cover-up

Finished Size: 46" x 61"

MATERIALS
Worsted Weight Yarn:
    39 ounces, (1,110 grams, 2,565 yards)
Crochet hook, size H (5.00 mm) **or** size needed
    for gauge
Yarn needle

GAUGE: Each Strip = 5½" wide x 59" long

Gauge Swatch: 4½" square
Work same as Strip through Row 5.

STITCH GUIDE

> **TREBLE CROCHET** *(abbreviated tr)*
> YO twice, insert hook in sp indicated, YO and pull up a loop (4 loops on hook), (YO and draw through 2 loops on hook) 3 times.
>
> **LONG SINGLE CROCHET** *(abbreviated LSC)*
> Working around loops of last 3 rows, insert hook in corner of diamond (ch-2 sp), YO and pull up a loop tall enough to allow loops to lay flat, YO and draw through both loops on hook.

STRIP (Make 8)
Ch 16 **loosely**.

Row 1: (2 Dc, ch 2, 3 dc) in fourth ch from hook, ch 6 **loosely**, skip next 5 chs, slip st in next ch, ch 2, **turn**; skip next slip st and first ch, dc in next 5 chs, ch 2, **turn**; dc in first 5 dc **(diamond made)**, ch 1, skip next ch-2 and next 5 chs, (3 dc, ch 2, 3 dc) in last ch.

Row 2 (Right side)**:** Turn; skip first dc, slip st in next 2 dc and in next ch-2 sp, ch 3, (2 dc, ch 2, 3 dc) in same sp, ch 10, skip next diamond, (3 dc, ch 2, 3 dc) in last ch-2 sp.

Note: Loop a short piece of yarn around any stitch to mark Row 2 as **right** side and bottom edge.

Rows 3 and 4: Turn; skip first dc, slip st in next 2 dc and in next ch-2 sp, ch 3, (2 dc, ch 2, 3 dc) in same sp, ch 10, (3 dc, ch 2, 3 dc) in last ch-2 sp; do **not** finish off.

Continued on page 7.

Row 5: Turn; skip first dc, slip st in next 2 dc and in next ch-2 sp, ch 3, (2 dc, ch 2, 3 dc) in same sp, ch 6 **loosely**, work LSC, ch 2, **turn**; skip next LSC and next ch, dc in next 5 chs, ch 2, **turn**; dc in first 5 dc **(diamond made)**, ch 1, (3 dc, ch 2, 3 dc) in last ch-2 sp.

Row 6: Turn; skip first dc, slip st in next 2 dc and in next ch-2 sp, ch 3, (2 dc, ch 2, 3 dc) in same sp, ch 10, skip next diamond, (3 dc, ch 2, 3 dc) in last ch-2 sp.

Rows 7 and 8: Turn; skip first dc, slip st in next 2 dc and in next ch-2 sp, ch 3, (2 dc, ch 2, 3 dc) in same sp, ch 10, (3 dc, ch 2, 3 dc) in last ch-2 sp.

Rows 9-81: Repeat Rows 5-8, 18 times; then repeat Row 5 once **more**.

Row 82: Turn; skip first dc, slip st in next 2 dc and in next ch-2 sp, ch 3, (dc, ch 3, slip st) in same sp, ch 5 **loosely**, slip st in corner of diamond, ch 5 **loosely**, (slip st, ch 3, dc, ch 3, slip st) in last ch-2 sp; do **not** finish off.

BORDER

Rnd 1: Ch 5, do **not** turn; † (dc in ch-2 sp on next row, ch 2) across long side *(Fig. 7)*, (3 dc, ch 2) twice in end of last row (corner); sc in next ch-5 sp, ch 1, [(dc, ch 1) twice, tr] in same sp, ch 1, tr in next ch-5 sp, ch 1, [(dc, ch 1) twice, sc] in same sp, ch 2; working across opposite side, (3 dc, ch 2) twice in end of first row †, dc in ch-2 sp on same row, ch 2, repeat from † to † once; join with slip st to third ch of beginning ch-5.

Fig. 7

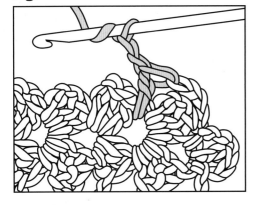

Rnd 2: Slip st in first ch-2 sp, ch 3, hdc in same sp, ★ (hdc, ch 1, hdc) in each ch-2 sp across to next corner, skip next dc, sc in next dc, (hdc, ch 1, hdc) in next ch-2 sp, skip next dc, sc in next dc, ch 2, skip next ch-2 sp, (hdc, ch 2, hdc) in next 7 ch-1 sps, ch 2, skip next ch-2 sp and next dc, sc in next dc, (hdc, ch 1, hdc) in next ch-2 sp, skip next dc, sc in next dc; repeat from ★ once **more**, (hdc, ch 1, hdc) in last ch-2 sp; join with slip st to second ch of beginning ch-3, finish off.

ASSEMBLY

Working through **inside** loops and holding bottom edges at same end, whipstitch Strips together beginning in first corner ch-1 and ending in next corner ch-1 *(Fig. 5b, page 2)*.

EDGING

Rnd 1: With **right** side facing, join yarn with slip st in top right corner ch-1 sp; ch 3, (dc, ch 1, 2 dc) in same sp, † dc in next sc and in next ch-2 sp, 2 dc in each of next 7 ch-2 sps, dc in next ch-2 sp, skip next sc, dc in next hdc, ★ dc in first hdc on next Strip, dc in next sc and in next ch-2 sp, 2 dc in each of next 7 ch-2 sps, dc in next ch-2 sp and in next sc, dc in next hdc; repeat from ★ across to last Strip, dc in first hdc on last Strip, skip next sc, dc in next ch-2 sp, 2 dc in each of next 7 ch-2 sps, dc in next ch-2 sp, skip next sc, dc in next hdc, (2 dc, ch 1, 2 dc) in next corner ch-1 sp, 3 dc in each ch-1 sp across to next corner ch-1 sp †, (2 dc, ch 1, 2 dc) in corner ch-1 sp, repeat from † to † once; join with slip st to top of beginning ch-3.

Rnd 2: Slip st in next dc and in next ch-1 sp, ch 3, (2 dc, ch 2, 3 dc) in same sp, ★ † skip next 5 dc, [(3 dc, ch 2, 3 dc) in next dc, skip next 4 dc] across to next corner ch-1 sp †, (3 dc, ch 2, 3 dc) in corner ch-1 sp; repeat from ★ 2 times **more**, then repeat from † to † once; join with slip st to top of beginning ch-3, finish off.

Design by Carol Alexander.

Delightfully Delicate

Finished Size: 50" x 71"

MATERIALS

Worsted Weight Brushed Acrylic Yarn:
  39 ounces, (1,110 grams, 3,010 yards)
Crochet hook, size J (6.00 mm) **or** size needed
  for gauge
Broomstick Lace Pin, size 50 (25.00 mm)

GAUGE: In pattern, one repeat (17 sts) = 5";
        Rows 1-8 = 4"

Gauge Swatch: 10"w x 7"h
Ch 35 **loosely**.
Work same as Afghan for 13 rows.
Finish off.

STITCH GUIDE

> **DECREASE** (uses next 2 sts)
> ★ YO, insert hook in **next** st, YO and pull up a loop,
> YO and draw through 2 loops on hook; repeat from
> ★ once **more**, YO and draw through all 3 loops on
> hook **(counts as one dc)**.
>
> **PUFF STITCH** (abbreviated Puff St)
> ★ YO, insert hook in st indicated, YO and pull up a
> loop even with loop on hook; repeat from ★ 3 times
> **more**, YO and draw through all 9 loops on hook.

AFGHAN

Ch 171 **loosely**.

Row 1: Dc in third ch from hook, decrease twice,
ch 1, (work Puff St in next ch, ch 1) 5 times,
★ decrease 6 times, ch 1, (work Puff St in next ch,
ch 1) 5 times; repeat from ★ across to last 6 chs,
decrease 3 times: 50 Puff Sts.

Row 2 (Right side)**:** Ch 1, turn; sc in each st and in each
ch-1 sp across to beginning ch-2, leave ch unworked:
170 sc.

Row 3: Ch 2, turn; dc in next sc, decrease twice,
ch 1, (work Puff St in next sc, ch 1) 5 times,
★ decrease 6 times, ch 1, (work Puff St in next sc,
ch 1) 5 times; repeat from ★ across to last 6 sc,
decrease 3 times.

Row 4: Ch 1, turn; sc in each st and in each ch-1 sp
across to beginning ch-2, leave ch unworked.

Rows 5-8: Repeat Rows 3 and 4 twice.

Row 9 (Broomstick lace)**:** Do **not** turn; slip loop from
hook onto pin **(Fig. 8)**, working from **left** to **right**, skip
first sc, ★ insert hook in next sc, YO and pull up a loop,
slip loop onto pin; repeat from ★ across: 170 loops.

Fig. 8

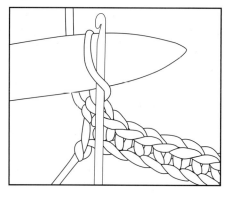

Row 10: Do **not** turn; insert hook from **left** to **right**
through first 3 loops on pin **(Fig. 9a)** and slip these
3 loops off, being careful not to tighten first loop, YO
and draw through all 3 loops on hook, ch 1 **(Fig. 9b)**,
work 3 sc in center of same 3 loops **(Fig. 9c)**, ★ insert
hook from **left** to **right** through next 4 loops on pin,
slip these 4 loops off and work 4 sc in center of same
4 loops; repeat from ★ across to last 3 loops on pin,
insert hook from **left** to **right** through last 3 loops,
slip these 3 loops off and work 3 sc in center of same
3 loops: 170 sc.

Fig. 9a   **Fig. 9b**

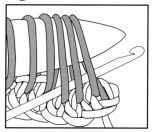 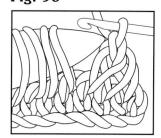

Fig. 9c

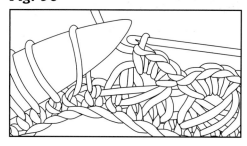

Row 11: Ch 1, **turn**; sc in each sc across.

Rows 12-20: Repeat Rows 9-11, 3 times.

Rows 21-28: Repeat Rows 3 and 4, 4 times.

Rows 29-148: Repeat Rows 9-28, 6 times.
Finish off.

Design by Maureen Egan Emlet.

Elegant in Ecru

Finished Size: 46" x 61"

MATERIALS
Cotton/Acrylic Blend Worsted Weight Yarn:
31½ ounces, (890 grams, 2,015 yards)
Crochet hook, size G (4.00 mm) **or** size needed
for gauge

GAUGE: In pattern, one repeat = 4"

Gauge Swatch: 4" square
Ch 18 **loosely.**
Row 1: Dc in fourth ch from hook **(3 skipped chs
count as first dc)** and in each ch across: 16 dc.
Rows 2-8: Ch 3 **(counts as first dc)**, turn; dc in next
dc and in each dc across.
Finish off.

STITCH GUIDE

SHELL
(3 Dc, ch 3, 3 dc) in ch indicated.

CLUSTER (uses next 3 dc)
★ YO, insert hook in **next** dc, YO and pull up a
loop, YO and draw through 2 loops on hook; repeat
from ★ 2 times **more**, YO and draw through all
4 loops on hook.

FRONT POST DOUBLE CROCHET
   (abbreviated FPdc)
YO, insert hook from **front** to **back** around post of
st indicated *(Fig. 4, page 2)*, YO and pull up a loop
(3 loops on hook), (YO and draw through 2 loops on
hook) twice. Skip st behind FPdc.

BACK POST DOUBLE CROCHET
   (abbreviated BPdc)
YO, insert hook from **back** to **front** around post of
st indicated *(Fig. 4, page 2)*, YO and pull up a loop
(3 loops on hook), (YO and draw through 2 loops on
hook) twice. Skip st in front of BPdc.

AFGHAN BODY
Ch 238 **loosely.**

Row 1 (Right side)**:** Slip st in eighth ch from hook, ch 2,
skip next ch, dc in next ch, ch 3, skip next 3 chs, dc in
next ch, ch 2, skip next ch, slip st in next ch, ch 2, skip
next ch, dc in next ch, ★ skip next 3 chs, work Shell in
next ch, skip next 3 chs, dc in next ch, ch 2, skip next
ch, slip st in next ch, ch 2, skip next ch, dc in next ch,
ch 3, skip next 3 chs, dc in next ch, ch 2, skip next ch,
slip st in next ch, ch 2, skip next ch, dc in next ch; repeat
from ★ across: 11 Shells.

Note: Loop a short piece of yarn around any stitch to
mark Row 1 as **right** side.

Row 2: Ch 6, turn; dc in next dc, ch 2, skip next ch,
slip st in next ch, ch 2, dc in next dc, ch 3, ★ dc in next
dc, work Cluster, ch 5, work Cluster, dc in next dc, ch 3,
dc in next dc, ch 2, skip next ch, slip st in next ch, ch 2,
dc in next dc, ch 3; repeat from ★ across to last 2 sps,
skip next ch-2 sp and next 2 chs, dc in next ch: 59 sps.

Row 3: Ch 5, turn; skip first ch, slip st in next ch, ch 2,
dc in next dc, ch 3, dc in next dc, ch 2, skip next ch,
slip st in next ch, ch 2, ★ dc in next dc, skip next 2 chs,
work Shell in next ch, skip next Cluster, dc in next dc,
ch 2, skip next ch, slip st in next ch, ch 2, dc in next dc,
ch 3, dc in next dc, ch 2, skip next ch, slip st in next ch,
ch 2; repeat from ★ across, skip next ch, dc in next ch:
11 Shells.

Rows 4-6: Repeat Rows 2 and 3 once, then repeat
Row 2 once **more**: 59 sps.

Row 7: Ch 5, turn; skip first ch, slip st in next ch, ch 2,
dc in next dc, ch 3, dc in next dc, ch 2, skip next ch,
slip st in next ch, ch 2, ★ dc in next dc, skip next Cluster
and next 2 chs, 6 dc in next ch, skip next Cluster, dc in
next dc, ch 2, skip next ch, slip st in next ch, ch 2, dc in
next dc, ch 3, dc in next dc, ch 2, skip next ch, slip st in
next ch, ch 2; repeat from ★ across, skip next ch, dc in
next ch: 60 sps.

Row 8: Ch 6, turn; dc in next dc, ch 2, skip next ch,
slip st in next ch, ch 2, dc in next dc, ch 3, ★ skip next
dc, (work FPdc around next dc, ch 3) 6 times, skip next
dc, dc in next dc, ch 2, skip next ch, slip st in next ch,
ch 2, dc in next dc, ch 3; repeat from ★ across to last
2 sps, skip next ch-2 sp and next 2 chs, dc in next ch:
103 sps.

Row 9: Ch 5, turn; skip first ch, slip st in next ch, ch 2,
dc in next dc, ch 3, dc in next dc, ★ work BPdc around
next FPdc, (ch 3, work BPdc around next FPdc) 5 times,
dc in next dc, ch 3, dc in next dc; repeat from ★ across
to last sp, ch 2, skip next ch, slip st in next ch, ch 2, skip
next ch, dc in next ch: 71 sps.

Row 10: Ch 6, turn; dc in next dc, ch 2, skip next ch,
slip st in next ch, ch 2, dc in next dc, ★ slip st in next
BPdc, [ch 3, skip next ch, (slip st, ch 5, slip st) in next ch,
ch 3, slip st in next BPdc] 5 times, dc in next dc, ch 2,
skip next ch, slip st in next ch, ch 2, dc in next dc; repeat
from ★ across to last 2 sps, ch 3, skip next ch-2 sp and
next 2 chs, dc in next ch: 191 sps.

Row 11: Ch 5, turn; skip first ch, slip st in next ch,
ch 2, ★ (dc in next dc, ch 3) twice, skip next 4 sps, sc
in next ch-5 sp, ch 3, (skip next 2 ch-3 sps, sc in next
ch-5 sp, ch 3) twice; repeat from ★ across to last 7 sps,
dc in next dc, ch 3, dc in next dc, ch 2, skip next ch,
slip st in next ch, ch 2, skip next ch, dc in next ch:
60 sps.

Row 12: Ch 6, turn; dc in next dc, ch 2, skip next ch, slip st in next ch, ch 2, dc in next dc, ch 3, ★ dc in next sc, work Shell in next sc, dc in next sc, ch 3, dc in next dc, ch 2, skip next ch, slip st in next ch, ch 2, dc in next dc, ch 3; repeat from ★ across to last 2 sps, skip next ch-2 sp and next 2 chs, dc in next ch: 11 Shells.

Row 13: Ch 5, turn; skip first ch, slip st in next ch, ch 2, dc in next dc, ch 3, dc in next dc, ch 2, skip next ch, slip st in next ch, ch 2, ★ dc in next dc, work Cluster, ch 5, work Cluster, dc in next dc, ch 2, skip next ch, slip st in next ch, ch 2, dc in next dc, ch 3, dc in next dc, ch 2, skip next ch, slip st in next ch, ch 2; repeat from ★ across, skip next ch, dc in next ch: 71 sps.

Row 14: Ch 6, turn; dc in next dc, ch 2, skip next ch, slip st in next ch, ch 2, dc in next dc, ch 3, ★ dc in next dc, skip next Cluster and next 2 chs, work Shell in next ch, skip next Cluster, dc in next dc, ch 3, dc in next dc, ch 2, skip next ch, slip st in next ch, ch 2, dc in next dc, ch 3; repeat from ★ across to last 2 sps, skip next ch-2 sp and next 2 chs, dc in next ch: 11 Shells.

Rows 15-17: Repeat Rows 13 and 14 once, then repeat Row 13 once **more**: 71 sps.

Row 18: Ch 6, turn; dc in next dc, ch 2, skip next ch, slip st in next ch, ch 2, dc in next dc, ch 3, ★ dc in next dc, skip next Cluster and next 2 chs, 6 dc in next ch, skip next Cluster, dc in next dc, ch 3, dc in next dc, ch 2, skip next ch, slip st in next ch, ch 2, dc in next dc, ch 3; repeat from ★ across to last 2 sps, skip next ch-2 sp and next 2 chs, dc in next ch: 48 sps.

Row 19: Ch 5, turn; skip first ch, slip st in next ch, ch 2, dc in next dc, ch 3, dc in next dc, ch 2, skip next ch, slip st in next ch, ch 2, ★ dc in next dc, work BPdc around next dc, (ch 3, work BPdc around next dc) 5 times, dc in next dc, ch 2, skip next ch, slip st in next ch, ch 2, dc in next dc, ch 3, dc in next dc, ch 2, skip next ch, slip st in next ch, ch 2; repeat from ★ across, skip next ch, dc in next ch: 115 sps.

Row 20: Ch 6, turn; dc in next dc, ch 2, skip next ch, slip st in next ch, ch 2, dc in next dc, ★ skip next dc, work FPdc around next BPdc, (ch 3, work FPdc around next BPdc) 5 times, skip next dc, dc in next dc, ch 2, skip next ch, slip st in next ch, ch 2, dc in next dc; repeat from ★ across to last 2 sps, ch 3, skip next ch-2 sp and next 2 chs, dc in next ch: 81 sps.

Row 21: Ch 5, turn; skip first ch, slip st in next ch, ch 2, dc in next dc, ch 3, dc in next dc, ★ slip st in next FPdc, [ch 3, skip next ch, (slip st, ch 5, slip st) in next ch, ch 3, slip st in next FPdc] 5 times, dc in next dc, ch 3, dc in next dc; repeat from ★ across to last sp, ch 2, skip next ch, slip st in next ch, ch 2, skip next ch, dc in next ch: 181 sps.

Row 22: Ch 6, turn; dc in next dc, ch 2, skip next ch, slip st in next ch, ch 2, dc in next dc, ch 3, ★ skip next 4 sps, sc in next ch-5 sp, ch 3, (skip next 2 ch-3 sps, sc in next ch-5 sp, ch 3) twice, dc in next dc, ch 2, skip next ch, slip st in next ch, ch 2, dc in next dc, ch 3; repeat from ★ across to last 2 sps, skip next ch-2 sp and next 2 chs, dc in next ch: 70 sps.

Row 23: Ch 5, turn; skip first ch, slip st in next ch, ch 2, dc in next dc, ch 3, dc in next dc, ch 2, skip next ch, slip st in next ch, ch 2, ★ dc in next sc, work Shell in next sc, dc in next sc, ch 2, skip next ch, slip st in next ch, ch 2, dc in next dc, ch 3, dc in next dc, ch 2, slip st in next ch, ch 2; repeat from ★ across, skip next ch, dc in next ch: 11 Shells.

Repeat Rows 2-23 for pattern until Afghan Body measures approximately 59", ending by working Row 10 **or** Row 21.

Finish off.

EDGING

Row 1: With **right** side facing and working in free loops of beginning ch *(Fig. 3b, page 1)*, join yarn with slip st in first ch; ch 5, skip next ch, slip st in next ch, ch 2, skip next ch, dc in next ch, ch 3, skip next 3 chs, dc in next ch, ch 2, skip next ch, slip st in next ch, ch 2, skip next ch, dc in next ch, ★ skip next 3 chs, 6 dc in next ch, skip next 3 chs, dc in next ch, ch 2, skip next ch, slip st in next ch, ch 2, skip next ch, dc in next ch, ch 3, skip next 3 chs, dc in next ch, ch 2, skip next ch, slip st in next ch, ch 2, skip next ch, dc in next ch; repeat from ★ 10 times **more**: 11 6-dc groups.

Rows 2-4: Work same as Rows 8-10 of Afghan.

Finish off.

Design by Rhonda Semonis.

Fresh as a Daisy

Finished Size: 48" x 63"

MATERIALS
Worsted Weight Brushed Acrylic Yarn:
  White - 27 ounces, (770 grams, 1,710 yards)
  Blue - 15 ounces, (430 grams, 950 yards)
  Yellow - 5 ounces, (140 grams, 315 yards)
Crochet hook, size I (5.50 mm) **or** size needed
  for gauge

GAUGE SWATCH: 5" square
Work same as First Square.

STITCH GUIDE

BEGINNING CLUSTER (uses one st)
Ch 2, ★ YO, insert hook in st indicated, YO and pull up a loop, YO and draw through 2 loops on hook; repeat from ★ once **more**, YO and draw through all 3 loops on hook.

CLUSTER (uses one st)
★ YO, insert hook in st indicated, YO and pull up a loop, YO and draw through 2 loops on hook; repeat from ★ 2 times **more**, YO and draw through all 4 loops on hook.

FIRST SQUARE
With Yellow, ch 4; join with slip st to form a ring.

Rnd 1 (Right side)**:** Ch 1, 12 sc in ring; join with slip st to first sc.

Note: Loop a short piece of yarn around any stitch to mark Rnd 1 as **right** side.

Rnd 2: Ch 1, sc in same st and in each sc around; join with slip st to first sc, finish off.

Rnd 3: With **right** side facing, join White with slip st in any sc; work Beginning Cluster in same st, ch 3, (work Cluster in next sc, ch 3) around; join with slip st to top of Beginning Cluster, finish off: 12 ch-3 sps.

Rnd 4: With **right** side facing, join Blue with slip st in any ch-3 sp; ch 3, (2 dc, ch 2, 3 dc) in same sp, 3 hdc in each of next 2 ch-3 sps, ★ (3 dc, ch 2, 3 dc) in next ch-3 sp, 3 hdc in each of next 2 ch-3 sps; repeat from ★ around; join with slip st to top of beginning ch-3, finish off: 48 sts and 4 ch-2 sps.

Rnd 5: With **right** side facing, join White with sc in any corner ch-2 sp *(see Joining With Sc, page 1)*; ch 6, sc in same sp, ch 4, (skip next 3 sts, sc in sp **before** next st, ch 4) 3 times, ★ (sc, ch 6, sc) in next corner ch-2 sp, ch 4, (skip next 3 sts, sc in sp **before** next st, ch 4) 3 times; repeat from ★ 2 times **more**; join with slip st to first sc, finish off: 20 sps.

ADDITIONAL SQUARES
Work same as First Square through Rnd 4: 48 sts and 4 ch-2 sps.

Rnd 5 (Joining rnd)**:** Work One or Two Side Joining forming 9 vertical strips of 12 Squares each.

Note: When working into corner ch-6 sp that has been previously joined, work into joining slip st.

ONE SIDE JOINING
Rnd 5 (Joining rnd)**:** With **right** side facing, join White with sc in any corner ch-2 sp; ch 4, (skip next 3 sts, sc in sp **before** next st, ch 4) 3 times, ★ (sc, ch 6, sc) in next corner ch-2 sp, ch 4, (skip next 3 sts, sc in sp **before** next st, ch 4) 3 times; repeat from ★ once **more**, sc in next corner ch-2 sp, ch 3, holding Squares with **wrong** sides together, slip st in corresponding corner ch-6 sp on **previous** Square, ch 3, sc in same corner sp on **new** Square, ch 2, slip st in next ch-4 sp on **previous** Square, ch 2, † skip next 3 sts on **new** Square, sc in sp **before** next st, ch 2, slip st in next ch-4 sp on **previous** Square, ch 2 †, repeat from † to † 2 times **more**, sc in same corner sp as first sc on **new** Square, ch 3, slip st in next corner ch-6 sp on **previous** Square, ch 3; join with slip st to first sc on **new** Square, finish off.

TWO SIDE JOINING
Rnd 5 (Joining rnd)**:** With **right** side facing, join White with sc in any corner ch-2 sp; ch 4, (skip next 3 sts, sc in sp **before** next st, ch 4) 3 times, (sc, ch 6, sc) in next corner ch-2 sp, ch 4, (skip next 3 sts, sc in sp **before** next st, ch 4) 3 times, sc in next corner ch-2 sp, ch 3, holding Squares with **wrong** sides together, ★ slip st in corresponding corner ch-6 sp on **previous** Square, ch 3, sc in same corner sp on **new** Square, ch 2, slip st in next ch-4 sp on **previous** Square, ch 2, † skip next 3 sts on **new** Square, sc in sp **before** next st, ch 2, slip st in next ch-4 sp on **previous** Square, ch 2 †, repeat from † to † 2 times **more**, sc in next corner ch-2 sp on **new** Square, ch 3; repeat from ★ once **more**, slip st in next corner ch-6 sp on **previous** Square, ch 3; join with slip st to first sc on **new** Square, finish off.

EDGING
Rnd 1: With **right** side facing, join White with sc in any corner ch-6 sp; ch 3, (dc, ch 3, dc) in next sp and in each sp across to next corner ch-6 sp, ch 3, ★ sc in corner ch-6 sp, ch 3, (dc, ch 3, dc) in next sp and in each sp across to next corner ch-6 sp, ch 3; repeat from ★ 2 times **more**; join with slip st to first sc.

Rnd 2: Slip st in first ch-3 sp, ch 6, slip st in second ch from hook, ch 1, dc in same sp, ★ dc in next ch-3 sp, ch 3, slip st in second ch from hook, ch 1, dc in same sp; repeat from ★ around; join with slip st to third ch of beginning ch-6, finish off.

Design by Martha Brooks Stein.

11

Granny's Granny

Finished Size: 53" x 63"

Note: We used 6 colors (Rose, Peach, Yellow, Green, Blue, and Purple) in light, medium, and dark shades to make our Afghan.

MATERIALS
Worsted Weight Yarn:
    Black - 21 ounces, (600 grams, 1,380 yards)
    3 Medium Shades - 3 ounces,
      (90 grams, 195 yards) **each**
    6 Light Shades - 2 ounces,
      (60 grams, 130 yards) **each**
    3 Medium Shades - 1½ ounces,
      (40 grams, 100 yards) **each**
    6 Dark Shades - 1 ounce,
      (30 grams, 65 yards) **each**
    Crochet hook, size K (6.50 mm) **or** size needed
      for gauge

GAUGE SWATCH: 5" square
Work same as First Square.

FIRST SQUARE

Note: Work First Square in shades of first color as indicated in either top corner square on Placement Diagram, page 13.

With dark shade, ch 4; join with slip st to form a ring.

Rnd 1 (Right side): Ch 3 **(counts as first dc, now and throughout)**, 2 dc in ring, ch 2, (3 dc in ring, ch 2) 3 times; join with slip st to first dc, finish off: 4 ch-2 sps.

Note: Loop a short piece of yarn around any stitch to mark Rnd 1 as **right** side.

Rnd 2: With **right** side facing, join medium shade with slip st in any ch-2 sp; ch 3, (2 dc, ch 2, 3 dc) in same sp, ch 1, ★ (3 dc, ch 2, 3 dc) in next ch-2 sp, ch 1; repeat from ★ 2 times **more**; join with slip st to first dc, finish off: 8 sps.

Rnd 3: With **right** side facing, join light shade with slip st in any corner ch-2 sp; ch 3, (2 dc, ch 2, 3 dc) in same sp, ch 1, 3 dc in next ch-1 sp, ch 1, ★ (3 dc, ch 2, 3 dc) in next corner ch-2 sp, ch 1, 3 dc in next ch-1 sp, ch 1; repeat from ★ 2 times **more**; join with slip st to first dc, finish off: 12 sps.

Rnd 4: With **right** side facing, join Black with slip st in any corner ch-2 sp; ch 3, (2 dc, ch 2, 3 dc) in same sp, ch 1, (3 dc in next ch-1 sp, ch 1) twice, ★ (3 dc, ch 2, 3 dc) in next corner ch-2 sp, ch 1, (3 dc in next ch-1 sp, ch 1) twice; repeat from ★ 2 times **more**; join with slip st to first dc, finish off: 16 sps.

ADDITIONAL SQUARES
Using shades of next color as indicated on Placement Diagram, work same as First Square through Rnd 3: 12 sps.

Rnd 4 (Joining rnd)**:** Using Placement Diagram as a guide, work One or Two Side Joining forming 9 vertical strips of 11 Squares each.

ONE SIDE JOINING
Rnd 4 (Joining rnd)**:** With **right** side facing, join Black with slip st in first ch-1 sp to **left** of any corner ch-2 sp; ch 3, 2 dc in same sp, ch 1, 3 dc in next ch-1 sp, ch 1, ★ (3 dc, ch 2, 3 dc) in next corner ch-2 sp, ch 1, (3 dc in next ch-1 sp, ch 1) twice; repeat from ★ once **more**, 3 dc in next corner ch-2 sp, ch 1, holding Squares with **wrong** sides together, sc in corner ch-2 sp on **previous Square**, ch 1, 3 dc in same sp on **new Square**, (sc in next ch-1 sp on **previous Square**, 3 dc in next sp on **new Square**) 3 times, ch 1, sc in next corner ch-2 sp on **previous Square**, ch 1, 3 dc in same corner sp on **new Square**, ch 1; join with slip st to first dc, finish off.

TWO SIDE JOINING
Rnd 4 (Joining rnd)**:** With **right** side facing, join Black with slip st in first ch-1 sp to **left** of any corner ch-2 sp; ch 3, 2 dc in same sp, ch 1, 3 dc in next ch-1 sp, ch 1, (3 dc, ch 2, 3 dc) in next corner ch-2 sp, ch 1, (3 dc in next sp, ch 1) 3 times, holding Squares with **wrong** sides together, sc in corner ch-2 sp on **previous Square**, † ch 1, 3 dc in same corner sp on **new Square**, (sc in next ch-1 sp on **previous Square**, 3 dc in next sp on **new Square**) 3 times, ch 1 †, sc in next corner ch-2 sp on **previous Square** and on **adjacent Square**, repeat from † to † once, sc in next corner ch-2 sp on **previous Square**, ch 1, 3 dc in same corner sp on **new Square**, ch 1; join with slip st to first dc, finish off.

Continued on page 13.

EDGING

Rnd 1: With **right** side facing, join Black with slip st in any corner ch-2 sp; ch 3, (2 dc, ch 2, 3 dc) in same sp, ch 1, (3 dc in next ch-1 sp, ch 1) 3 times, † dc in next sp, dc in next joining and in sp on next Square, ch 1, (3 dc in next ch-1 sp, ch 1) 3 times †, repeat from † to † across to next corner ch-2 sp, ★ (3 dc, ch 2, 3 dc) in corner ch-2 sp, ch 1, (3 dc in next ch-1 sp, ch 1) 3 times, repeat from † to † across to next corner ch-2 sp; repeat from ★ 2 times **more**; join with slip st to first dc, finish off: 164 sps.

Rnd 2: With **right** side facing, join any medium shade with slip st in any corner ch-2 sp; ch 3, (2 dc, ch 2, 3 dc) in same sp, ch 1, (3 dc in next ch-1 sp, ch 1) across to next corner ch-2 sp, ★ (3 dc, ch 2, 3 dc) in corner ch-2 sp, ch 1, (3 dc in next ch-1 sp, ch 1) across to next corner ch-2 sp; repeat from ★ 2 times **more**; join with slip st to first dc, finish off: 168 sps.

Rnd 3: With **right** side facing, join Black with slip st in any corner ch-2 sp; ch 3, (2 dc, ch 2, 3 dc) in same sp, ch 1, (3 dc in next ch-1 sp, ch 1) across to next corner ch-2 sp, ★ (3 dc, ch 2, 3 dc) in corner ch-2 sp, ch 1, (3 dc in next ch-1 sp, ch 1) across to next corner ch-2 sp; repeat from ★ 2 times **more**; join with slip st to first dc, finish off: 172 sps.

Rnds 4-7: Repeat Rnds 2 and 3 twice; at the end of Rnd 7, do **not** finish off: 188 sps.

Rnd 8: Slip st in next 2 dc and in next corner ch-2 sp, ch 1, sc in same sp, ★ † ch 2, sc in next dc, ch 2, skip next dc, sc in next dc, ch 2, (skip next ch-1 sp, sc in next dc, ch 2, skip next dc, sc in next dc, ch 2) across to next corner ch-2 sp †, sc in corner ch-2 sp; repeat from ★ 2 times **more**, then repeat from † to † once; join with slip st to first sc, finish off.

Design by Martha Brooks Stein.

PLACEMENT DIAGRAM

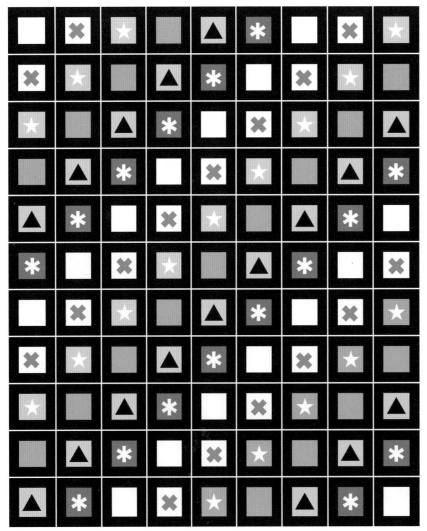

KEY

☐ - Rose

☒ - Peach

⬚ - Yellow

▦ - Green

▲ - Blue

✳ - Purple

Handsome for Him

Finished Size: 50" x 72"

MATERIALS
Worsted Weight Yarn:
Black - 31 ounces, (880 grams, 1,905 yards)
Grey - 22 ounces, (620 grams, 1,350 yards)
Crochet hook, size J (6.00 mm) **or** size needed for gauge
Yarn needle

GAUGE: In pattern, 7 dc and 3 rows = 1¾"
Each Panel = 5½" wide

Gauge Swatch: 3¼"w x 4"h
Work same as Panel through Row 5 of Diamonds.

STITCH GUIDE

TREBLE CROCHET *(abbreviated tr)*
YO twice, insert hook in st or sp indicated, YO and pull up a loop (4 loops on hook), (YO and draw through 2 loops on hook) 3 times.

DECREASE *(uses next 2 sts or sps)*
★ YO twice, insert hook in **next** st or sp, YO and pull up a loop, (YO and draw through 2 loops on hook) twice; repeat from ★ once **more**, YO and draw through all 3 loops on hook **(counts as one tr)**.

PANEL (Make 9)
DIAMONDS
With Black, ch 14 **loosely**.

Row 1 (Right side)**:** Dc in sixth ch from hook, ★ ch 1, skip next ch, dc in next ch; repeat from ★ across: 5 sps.

Note: Loop a short piece of yarn around any stitch to mark Row 1 as **right** side and bottom edge.

Row 2: Ch 4 **(counts as first dc plus ch 1)**, turn; dc in next dc, (dc in next ch-1 sp and in next dc) 3 times, ch 1, skip next ch, dc in next ch.

Rows 3 and 4: Ch 4 **(counts as first dc plus ch 1)**, turn; dc in next 7 dc, ch 1, dc in last dc.

Row 5: Ch 4 **(counts as first dc plus ch 1)**, turn; dc in next dc, ch 1, ★ skip next dc, dc in next dc, ch 1; repeat from ★ 2 times **more**, dc in last dc.

Row 6: Turn; slip st **loosely** in each dc and in each ch-1 sp across.

Row 7: Ch 14 **loosely**; dc in sixth ch from hook, ★ ch 1, skip next ch, dc in next ch; repeat from ★ 3 times **more**, leave remaining sts unworked: 5 sps.

Rows 8-107: Repeat Rows 2-7, 16 times; then repeat Rows 2 5 once **more**: 18 Diamonds.

Finish off.

SIDE
Row 1: With **wrong** side facing and working across one side of all Diamonds, join Grey with slip st in first sp at either point; ch 4 **(counts as first tr, now and throughout)**, 2 tr in next sp, 2 dc in next sp, 2 hdc in next sp, 2 sc in next sp, 2 hdc in next sp, ★ 2 dc in each of next 2 sps, decrease working in next 2 sps, 2 dc in each of next 2 sps, 2 hdc in next sp, 2 sc in next sp, 2 hdc in next sp; repeat from ★ across to last 3 sps, 2 dc in next sp, 2 tr in next sp, tr in last sp: 271 sts.

Row 2: Ch 4, turn; decrease in next 2 tr, tr in next dc, dc in next 2 sts, hdc in next hdc, sc in next 2 sc, hdc in next hdc, ★ dc in next 3 sts, decrease in next 2 dc, tr in next tr, decrease in next 2 dc, dc in next 3 sts, hdc in next hdc, sc in next 2 sc, hdc in next hdc; repeat from ★ across to last 6 sts, dc in next 2 sts, tr in next dc, decrease in next 2 tr, tr in last tr; finish off: 235 sts.

Row 3: With **right** side facing, join Black with slip st in first tr; ch 3, dc in next st and in each st across; finish off.

Repeat for second side.

ASSEMBLY
With Black, working through **both** loops, and holding bottom edges at same end, whipstitch Panels together beginning in first st and ending in last st *(Fig. 5a, page 2)*.

Holding 5 strands of Black yarn together, each 16" long, add fringe in each row across short edges of Afghan *(Figs. 6c & d, page 2)*.

Design by Terry Kimbrough.

Irresistible Ripple

Finished Size: 48" x 62"

MATERIALS

Worsted Weight Yarn:
    Off-White - 36 ounces, (1,020 grams, 2,100 yards)
    Green - 12 ounces, (340 grams, 700 yards)
    Rose - 10 ounces, (280 grams, 585 yards)
Crochet hook, size P (10.00 mm) **or** size needed
    for gauge

Note: Afghan is worked holding two strands of yarn together.

GAUGE: In pattern, one repeat = 6"; 6 rows = 7"

Gauge Swatch 12"w x 7"h
Ch 37 **loosely**.
Work same as Afghan Body for 6 rows.
Finish off.

STITCH GUIDE

DECREASE (uses next 5 sts)
† YO, insert hook in **next** st, YO and pull up a loop, YO and draw through 2 loops on hook †, skip next 3 sts, repeat from † to † once, YO and draw through all 3 loops on hook **(counts as one dc)**.

ENDING DECREASE (uses last 3 sts)
† YO, insert hook in **next** st, YO and pull up a loop, YO and draw through 2 loops on hook †, skip next st, repeat from † to † once, YO and draw through all 3 loops on hook **(counts as one dc)**.

AFGHAN BODY

With Off-White, ch 157 **loosely**.

Row 1: Dc in fifth ch from hook **(4 skipped chs count as first dc plus ch 1)**, ch 1, skip next ch, (dc in next ch, ch 1, skip next ch) twice, (dc, ch 3, dc) in next ch, ch 1, ★ skip next ch, (dc in next ch, ch 1, skip next ch) 3 times, decrease, ch 1, skip next ch, (dc in next ch, ch 1, skip next ch) 3 times, (dc, ch 3, dc) in next ch, ch 1; repeat from ★ across to last 6 chs, skip next ch, (dc in next ch, ch 1, skip next ch) twice, (dc, ch 1, dc) in last ch: 73 dc.

Row 2 (Right side)**:** Ch 2, turn; dc in next dc, (dc in next ch-1 sp and in next dc) 3 times, (2 dc, ch 3, 2 dc) in next ch-3 sp, (dc in next dc and in next ch-1 sp) 3 times, ★ decrease, (dc in next ch-1 sp and in next dc) 3 times, (2 dc, ch 3, 2 dc) in next ch-3 sp, (dc in next dc and in next ch-1 sp) 3 times; repeat from ★ across to last 2 dc, work ending decrease: 137 dc.

*Note: Loop a short piece of yarn around any stitch to mark Row 2 as **right** side.*

Row 3: Ch 2, turn; skip first 2 dc, dc in next dc, ch 1, (skip next dc, dc in next dc, ch 1) 3 times, (dc, ch 3, dc) in next ch-3 sp, ch 1, dc in next dc, ch 1, (skip next dc, dc in next dc, ch 1) twice, ★ skip next dc, decrease, ch 1, (skip next dc, dc in next dc, ch 1) 3 times, (dc, ch 3, dc) in next ch-3 sp, ch 1, dc in next dc, ch 1, (skip next dc, dc in next dc, ch 1) twice; repeat from ★ across to last 4 dc, skip next dc, work ending decrease: 73 dc.

Row 4: Ch 2, turn; dc in next dc, (dc in next ch-1 sp and in next dc) 3 times, (2 dc, ch 3, 2 dc) in next ch-3 sp, (dc in next dc and in next ch-1 sp) 3 times, ★ decrease, (dc in next ch-1 sp and in next dc) 3 times, (2 dc, ch 3, 2 dc) in next ch-3 sp, (dc in next dc and in next ch-1 sp) 3 times; repeat from ★ across to last 2 dc, work ending decrease changing to Green *(Fig. 2a, page 1)*: 137 dc.

Row 5: Repeat Row 3 changing to Rose in last dc.

Row 6: Repeat Row 4 changing to Off-White in last dc.

Row 7: Repeat Row 3.

Row 8: Ch 2, turn; dc in next dc, (dc in next ch-1 sp and in next dc) 3 times, (2 dc, ch 3, 2 dc) in next ch-3 sp, (dc in next dc and in next ch-1 sp) 3 times, ★ decrease, (dc in next ch-1 sp and in next dc) 3 times, (2 dc, ch 3, 2 dc) in next ch-3 sp, (dc in next dc and in next ch-1 sp) 3 times; repeat from ★ across to last 2 dc, work ending decrease: 137 dc.

Rows 9-52: Repeat Rows 3-8, 7 times; then repeat Rows 3 and 4 once **more**; at the end of Row 52, do **not** change colors.

Finish off.

EDGING

With **right** side facing, join Green with sc in first dc *(see Joining With Sc, page 1)*; skip next 2 dc, 5 dc in next dc, skip next 2 dc, sc in next dc, 7 dc in next ch-3 sp, skip next 2 dc, sc in next dc, † (skip next 2 dc, 5 dc in next dc, skip next 2 dc, sc in next dc) twice, 7 dc in next ch-3 sp, skip next 2 dc, sc in next dc †, repeat from † to † across to last 6 dc, skip next 2 dc, 5 dc in next dc, skip next 2 dc, sc in last dc; working in end of rows, (5 dc, sc) in first row, (5 dc in next row, sc in next row) across to last row, 7 dc in last row; working in sps and in free loops across beginning ch *(Fig. 3b, page 1)*, sc in ch at base of first dc, (skip next 2 chs, 5 dc in next ch, skip next 2 chs, sc in next ch) twice, ★ 7 dc in next ch-3 sp, skip next 2 chs, sc in next ch, (skip next 2 chs, 5 dc in next ch, skip next 2 chs, sc in next ch) twice; repeat from ★ across; working in end of rows, 7 dc in first row, (sc in next row, 5 dc in next row) across to last row, (sc, 5 dc) in last row; join with slip st to first sc, finish off.

Design by Carole Prior.

Just Blues

Finished Size: 53½" x 64½"

MATERIALS
Worsted Weight Yarn:
  Blue - 15 ounces, (430 grams, 1,115 yards)
  White - 11 ounces, (310 grams, 815 yards)
  Dk Blue - 9 ounces, (260 grams, 670 yards)
  Lt Blue - 7 ounces, (200 grams, 520 yards)
  Crochet hook, size J (6.00 mm) **or** size needed
    for gauge

GAUGE: In pattern, 13 sts = 4"; 16 rows = 9"

Gauge Swatch: 4¼"w x 9"h
Ch 15 **loosely**.
Work same as Afghan for 16 rows.
Finish off.

Note: Each row is worked across length of Afghan.

STITCH GUIDE

TREBLE CROCHET *(abbreviated tr)*
YO twice, insert hook in st indicated, YO and pull
up a loop (4 loops on hook), (YO and draw through
2 loops on hook) 3 times.

CLUSTER (uses next 3 sts)
★ YO, insert hook in **next** st, YO and pull up a loop,
YO and draw through 2 loops on hook; repeat from
★ 2 times **more**, YO and draw through all 4 loops
on hook.

AFGHAN
With Blue, ch 210 **loosely**.

Row 1 (Right side): Sc in second ch from hook and in
each ch across changing to White in last sc *(Fig. 2a,
page 1)*: 209 sc.

Note: Loop a short piece of yarn around any stitch to
mark Row 1 as **right** side.

Row 2: Ch 3 **(counts as first dc, now and
throughout)**, turn; skip next sc, 3 dc in next sc, (skip
next 2 sc, 3 dc in next sc) across to last 2 sc, skip next sc,
dc in last sc: 69 3-dc groups.

Row 3: Ch 4 **(counts as first dc plus ch 1)**, turn;
working in Back Loops Only *(Fig. 1, page 1)*, work
Cluster, (ch 2, work Cluster) across to last dc, ch 1, dc in
last dc changing to Blue: 70 sps.

Row 4: Ch 1, turn; working in both loops, 2 sc in
first ch-1 sp, (sc in next Cluster, 2 sc in next sp) across
changing to Lt Blue in last sc: 209 sc.

Row 5: Ch 3, turn; skip next sc, 3 dc in next sc, (skip
next 2 sc, 3 dc in next sc) across to last 2 sc, skip next sc,
dc in last sc changing to Blue: 69 3-dc groups.

Row 6: Ch 1, turn; sc in Back Loop Only of each dc
across changing to Dk Blue in last sc: 209 sc.

Row 7: Ch 4 **(counts as first tr)**, turn; tr in Back
Loop Only of next sc and each sc across.

Row 8: Ch 4 **(counts as first tr)**, turn; tr in both loops
of next tr and each tr across.

Row 9: Ch 4 **(counts as first tr)**, turn; tr in next tr
and in each tr across changing to Blue in last tr.

Row 10: Ch 1, turn; sc in Back Loop Only of each tr
across changing to Lt Blue in last sc.

Row 11: Ch 4 **(counts as first dc plus ch 1)**, turn;
working in Back Loops Only, work Cluster, (ch 2, work
Cluster) across to last sc, ch 1, dc in last sc changing to
Blue: 70 sps.

Row 12: Ch 1, turn; working in both loops, 2 sc in
first ch-1 sp, (sc in next Cluster, 2 sc in next sp) across
changing to White in last sc: 209 sc.

Row 13: Ch 3, turn; skip next sc, 3 dc in next sc, (skip
next 2 sc, 3 dc in next sc) across to last 2 sc, skip next sc,
dc in last sc: 69 3-dc groups.

Row 14: Ch 4 **(counts as first dc plus ch 1)**, turn;
working in Front Loops Only, work Cluster, (ch 2, work
Cluster) across to last dc, ch 1, dc in last dc changing to
Blue: 70 sps.

Row 15: Ch 1, turn; working in both loops, 2 sc in
first ch-1 sp, (sc in next Cluster, 2 sc in next sp) across
changing to Lt Blue in last sc: 209 sc.

Row 16: Ch 4 **(counts as first tr)**, turn; tr in Front
Loop Only of next sc and each sc across changing to
Blue in last tr.

Row 17: Ch 1, turn; sc in both loops of each tr across
changing to White in last sc.

Rows 18-95: Repeat Rows 2-17, 4 times; then repeat
Rows 2-15 once **more**; at end of Row 95, do **not**
change colors.

Finish off.

Holding 6 strands of Blue yarn together, each 16" long,
add fringe evenly spaced across end of rows on short
edges of Afghan *(Figs. 6c & d, page 2)*, using photo,
page 21, as a guide for placement.

Design by Nancy Fuller.

Kid-Pleasing Comfort

Finished Size: 45" x 60"

MATERIALS

Worsted Weight Yarn:
Blue - 45 ounces, (1,280 grams, 2,545 yards)
Red - 5 ounces, (140 grams, 285 yards)
Yellow - 2 ounces, (60 grams, 115 yards)
Green - 1½ ounces, (40 grams, 85 yards)
Fuchsia - ¾ ounce, (20 grams, 45 yards)
Orange - ½ ounce, (15 grams, 30 yards)
White - 3 yards
Black - 2 yards
Afghan hook, size J (6.00 mm) **or** size needed
for gauge
Crochet hook, size H (5.00 mm) **or** size needed
for gauge
Yarn needle

GAUGE: In Afghan St, 16 sts and 14 rows = 4"
Block before Edging = 13" square
Edging, 16 sc = 4"

Gauge Swatch: 4" square
With afghan hook, ch 17 **loosely**.
Work same as Basic Block for 14 rows.
Finish off.

STITCH GUIDE

AFGHAN STITCH *(abbreviated Afghan St)*
With yarn in **back**, insert hook from **right** to **left**
under next vertical strand *(Fig. 10)*, YO and pull up
a loop.

Fig. 10

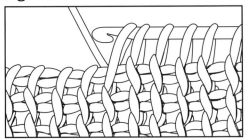

PUFF STITCH *(abbreviated Puff St)*
YO, insert hook from **right** to **left** under **both**
vertical strands of next st *(Fig. 11)*, YO and pull up
a loop, ★ YO, insert hook from **right** to **left** under
both vertical strands of same st, YO and pull up
a loop; repeat from ★ once **more**, YO and draw
through first 6 loops on hook, ch 1 to close.

Fig. 11

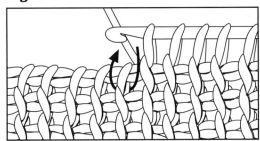

BASIC BLOCK (Make 6)

With afghan hook and Blue, ch 52 **loosely**.

Note: Each row is worked in 2 steps, working to the **left** picking up loops and then working to the **right** completing each stitch.

Row 1 (Right side): Working from **right** to **left** and in Top Loops Only, insert hook in second ch from hook, YO and pull up a loop (2 loops on hook), pull up a loop in each ch across *(Fig. 12a)* (52 loops on hook); working from **left** to **right**, YO and draw through first loop on hook, ★ YO and draw through 2 loops on hook *(Fig. 12b)*; repeat from ★ across until one loop remains on hook. This is the first stitch of the next row.

Fig. 12a   **Fig. 12b**

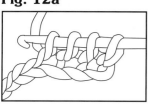   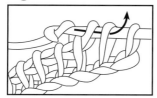

Note: Loop a short piece of yarn around any stitch to mark Row 1 as **right** side and bottom edge.

Rows 2-46: Working from **right** to **left**, skip first vertical strand, work Afghan Sts across *(Fig. 10, page 17)* (52 loops on hook); working from **left** to **right**, YO and draw through first loop on hook, (YO and draw through 2 loops on hook) across.

Last Row: Working from **right** to **left**, skip first vertical strand, ★ insert hook under next vertical strand, YO and draw **loosely** through strand **and** loop on hook *(Fig. 13)*; repeat from ★ across; do **not** finish off.

Fig. 13

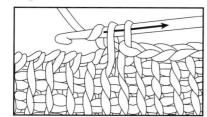

EDGING

Rnd 1: With crochet hook, ch 1, sc in end of each row across; working in free loops of beginning ch *(Fig. 3b, page 1)*, 3 sc in first ch, work 46 sc evenly spaced across to last ch, 3 sc in last ch; sc in end of each row across; working across last row, 3 sc in first st, work 46 sc evenly spaced across to last st, 3 sc in last st; join with slip st to first sc: 196 sc.

Rnd 2: Ch 1, sc in each sc around working 3 sc in center sc of each corner 3-sc group; join with slip st to first sc, finish off: 204 sc.

TEXTURED BLOCK (Make 6)

With afghan hook and Blue, ch 52 **loosely**.

Rows 1-16: Work same as Basic Block.

Row 17: Working from **right** to **left**, skip first vertical strand, work 25 Afghan Sts, work Puff St *(Fig. 11, page 17)*, work Afghan Sts across; working from **left** to **right**, YO and draw through first loop on hook, (YO and draw through 2 loops on hook) across.

Row 18: Working from **right** to **left**, skip first vertical strand, work 22 Afghan Sts, work Puff St, work 5 Afghan Sts, work Puff St, work Afghan Sts across; working from **left** to **right**, YO and draw through first loop on hook, (YO and draw through 2 loops on hook) across.

Row 19: Working from **right** to **left**, skip first vertical strand, work 19 Afghan Sts, work Puff St, (work 5 Afghan Sts, work Puff St) twice, work Afghan Sts across; working from **left** to **right**, YO and draw through first loop on hook, (YO and draw through 2 loops on hook) across.

Row 20: Working from **right** to **left**, skip first vertical strand, work 16 Afghan Sts, work Puff St, (work 5 Afghan Sts, work Puff St) 3 times, work Afghan Sts across; working from **left** to **right**, YO and draw through first loop on hook, (YO and draw through 2 loops on hook) across.

Row 21: Working from **right** to **left**, skip first vertical strand, work 13 Afghan Sts, work Puff St, (work 5 Afghan Sts, work Puff St) 4 times, work Afghan Sts across; working from **left** to **right**, YO and draw through first loop on hook, (YO and draw through 2 loops on hook) across; do **not** finish off.

Continued on page 19.

Row 22: Working from **right** to **left**, skip first vertical strand, work 10 Afghan Sts, work Puff St, (work 5 Afghan Sts, work Puff St) 5 times, work Afghan Sts across; working from **left** to **right**, YO and draw through first loop on hook, (YO and draw through 2 loops on hook) across.

Row 23: Working from **right** to **left**, skip first vertical strand, work 7 Afghan Sts, work Puff St, (work 5 Afghan Sts, work Puff St) 6 times, work Afghan Sts across; working from **left** to **right**, YO and draw through first loop on hook, (YO and draw through 2 loops on hook) across.

Rows 24-26: Repeat Rows 22 and 23 once, then repeat Row 22 once **more**.

Row 27: Repeat Row 21.

Row 28: Repeat Row 20.

Row 29: Repeat Row 19.

Row 30: Repeat Row 18.

Row 31: Repeat Row 17.

Rows 32-46: Working from **right** to **left**, skip first vertical strand, work Afghan Sts across; working from **left** to **right**, YO and draw through first loop on hook, (YO and draw through 2 loops on hook) across.

Row 47: Working from **right** to **left**, skip first vertical strand, ★ insert hook under next vertical strand, YO and draw **loosely** through strand **and** loop on hook; repeat from ★ across; do **not** finish off.

EDGING
Work same as Basic Block, page 18.

FINISHING
CROSS STITCH
Following charts and referring to Placement Diagram, cross stitch dinosaurs in center of Blocks as follows: Each square on the chart represents one complete cross stitch. Cross stitches are worked over the upright bar of the Afghan Stitch **(Fig. 14)**. If you find it difficult to see where to work the cross stitches, hold the Block at each side and pull slightly. Evenly spaced holes will be apparent on each side of the upright bars.

Fig. 14

Thread a yarn needle with an 18" strand of yarn. Hold Block with **right** side facing and marked edge at bottom. Count to find bar where you wish to begin. Bring needle up from back of Block through first hole, leaving a 3" end on back. Work over this end to secure. Bring needle down through hole diagonally across, pulling yarn flat against Block, but not so tight as to cause a pucker. You have now made one half of a cross stitch. You can either

complete the stitch now, or work across an area in half crosses and then work back, crossing them as you go. Just be sure that the top half of every cross stitch is worked in the same direction.

Finish off by weaving end of yarn under several stitches; cut close to work.

BRONTOSAURUS

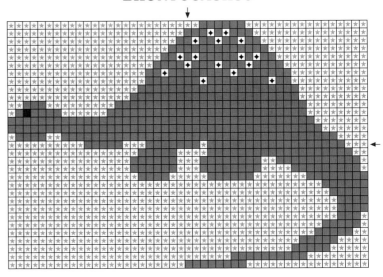

TRICERATOPS

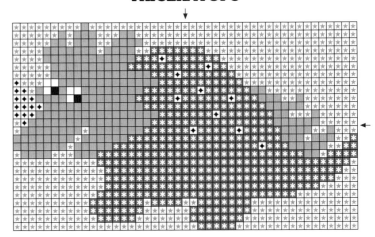

STEGOSAURUS

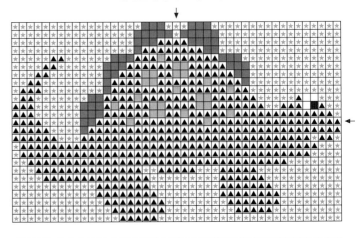

KEY		
□ - White	✳ - Red	▲ - Purple
✦ - Yellow	⬚ - Blue	■ - Black
▨ - Orange	▦ - Green	

19

ASSEMBLY

With Blue, working through **both** loops, and following Placement Diagram as a guide, whipstitch Blocks together forming 3 vertical strips of 4 Blocks each *(Fig. 5a, page 2)*, beginning in center sc of first corner 3-sc group and ending in center sc of next corner 3-sc group; then whipstitch strips together in same manner.

BORDER

Rnd 1: With **right** side facing, join Yellow with slip st in center sc of any corner 3-sc group; ch 1, sc evenly around entire Afghan working 3 sc in center sc of each corner 3-sc group; join with slip st to first sc.

Rnd 2: Ch 1, turn; sc in same st and in each sc around working 3 sc in center sc of each corner 3-sc group; join with slip st to first sc changing to Red *(Fig. 2b, page 1)*.

Rnds 3-6: Ch 1, turn; sc in same st and in each sc around working 3 sc in center sc of each corner 3-sc group; join with slip st to first sc.

Rnd 7: Turn; slip st in each sc around; join with slip st to first slip st, finish off.

PLACEMENT DIAGRAM

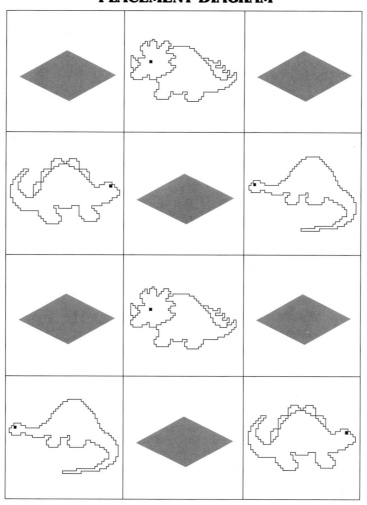

All American

Just
Blues

Zest for the
West

22

Delightfully Delicate

Elegant in Ecru

Handsome for Him

Fresh as a Daisy

Classic Cover-up

Sweet Dreams

Irresistible Ripple

Marvelous Mile-a-Minute

Old Fashioned Favorite

Pretty in Peach

Bold Beauty

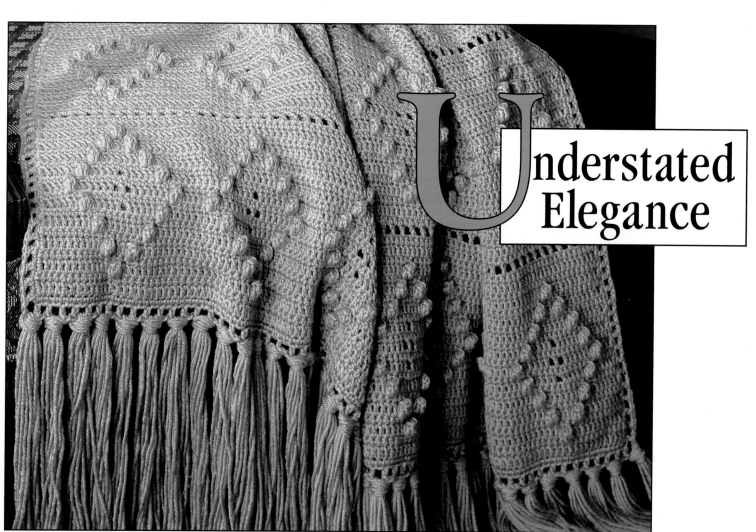

Understated Elegance

Granny's Granny

Quick & Easy Choices

Naturally
Nice

Winter
Warmers

Very Victorian

Young at Heart

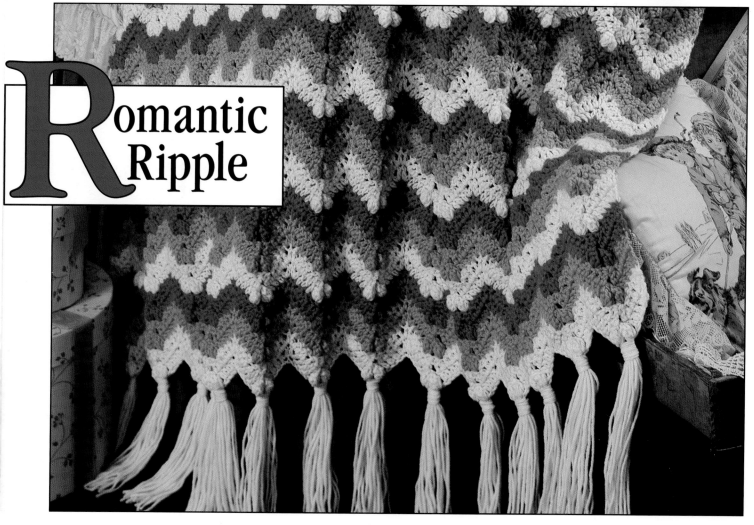

Romantic Ripple

Lovely Lace

Finished Size: 45" x 55"

MATERIALS
Worsted Weight Yarn:
   50 ounces, (1,420 grams, 3,165 yards)
   Crochet hook, size I (5.50 mm) **or** size needed
      for gauge

GAUGE SWATCH: 5" square
Work same as First Motif.

STITCH GUIDE

PICOT
Ch 5, sc in fourth ch from hook.

CORNER PICOT
Ch 6, sc in fourth ch from hook.

FIRST MOTIF
Ch 7; join with slip st to form a ring.

Rnd 1 (Right side)**:** Ch 1, 16 sc in ring; join with slip st to first sc.

Note: Loop a short piece of yarn around any stitch to mark Rnd 1 as **right** side.

Rnd 2: Ch 1, sc in same st, ch 2, skip next sc, ★ sc in next sc, ch 2, skip next sc; repeat from ★ around; join with slip st to first sc: 8 ch-2 sps.

Rnd 3: Slip st in first ch-2 sp, ch 1, (sc, 3 dc, sc) in same sp, ch 1, ★ (sc, 3 dc, sc) in next ch-2 sp, ch 1; repeat from ★ around; join with slip st to first sc: 8 petals.

Rnd 4: Slip st in next 2 dc, ch 1, sc in same st, ★ † ch 3, (hdc, ch 1, hdc) in next ch-1 sp, ch 3, sc in center dc of next 3-dc group †, ch 4, sc in center dc of next 3-dc group; repeat from ★ 2 times **more**, then repeat from † to † once, ch 2, hdc in first sc to form last ch-4 sp: 16 sps.

Rnd 5: Ch 3 **(counts as first dc, now and throughout)**, 2 dc in same sp, ch 4, skip next ch-3 sp, sc in next 3 sts, ch 4, skip next ch-3 sp, ★ (3 dc, ch 3, 3 dc) in next ch-4 sp, ch 4, skip next ch-3 sp, sc in next 3 sts, ch 4, skip next ch-3 sp; repeat from ★ 2 times **more**, 3 dc in same sp as first dc, ch 3; join with slip st to first dc.

Rnd 6: Ch 3, dc in next 2 dc, ★ † ch 5, slip st in next sc, work Picot, ch 1, skip next sc, slip st in next sc, ch 5, dc in next 3 dc, work Corner Picot, ch 2 †, dc in next 3 dc; repeat from ★ 2 times **more**, then repeat from † to † once; join with slip st to first dc, finish off.

ADDITIONAL MOTIFS
Work same as First Motif through Rnd 5.

Rnd 6 (Joining rnd)**:** Work One or Two Side Joining forming 9 vertical strips of 11 Motifs each.

Note: When working into Corner Picot that has been previously joined, work into same ch.

ONE SIDE JOINING
Rnd 6 (Joining rnd)**:** Ch 3, dc in next 2 dc, ★ † ch 5, slip st in next sc, work Picot, ch 1, skip next sc, slip st in next sc, ch 5, dc in next 3 dc †, work Corner Picot, ch 2, dc in next 3 dc; repeat from ★ once **more**, then repeat from † to † once, ch 2, holding Motifs with **wrong** sides together, slip st in center ch of corresponding Corner Picot on **previous Motif**, ch 2, dc in next 3 dc on **new Motif**, ch 1, slip st in second ch of next ch-5 on **previous Motif**, ch 3, skip next ch-4 sp on **new Motif**, slip st in next sc, ch 1, slip st in center ch of next Picot on **previous Motif**, ch 1, skip next sc on **new Motif**, slip st in next sc, ch 3, slip st in fourth ch of next ch-5 on **previous Motif**, ch 1, dc in next 3 dc on **new Motif**, ch 2, slip st in center ch of next Corner Picot on **previous Motif**, ch 2; join with slip st to first dc on **new Motif**, finish off.

TWO SIDE JOINING

Rnd 6 (Joining rnd)**:** Ch 3, dc in next 2 dc, † ch 5, slip st in next sc, work Picot, ch 1, skip next sc, slip st in next sc, ch 5, dc in next 3 dc †, work Corner Picot, ch 2, dc in next 3 dc, repeat from † to † once, ch 2, holding Motifs with **wrong** sides together, slip st in center ch of corresponding Corner Picot on **previous Motif**, ch 2, ★ dc in next 3 dc on **new Motif**, ch 1, slip st in second ch of next ch-5 sp on **previous Motif**, ch 3, skip next ch-4 sp on **new Motif**, slip st in next sc, ch 1, slip st in center ch of next Picot on **previous Motif**, ch 1, skip next sc on **new Motif**, slip st in next sc, ch 3, slip st in fourth ch of next ch-5 on **previous Motif**, ch 1, dc in next 3 dc on **new Motif**, ch 2, slip st in center ch of next Corner Picot on **previous Motif**, ch 2; repeat from ★ once **more**; join with slip st to first dc on **new Motif**, finish off.

TASSELS

Add tassels in each corner and in each joining across short edges of Afghan as follows:

Cut a piece of cardboard 3" wide x 8" long. Wind a double strand of yarn around the cardboard lengthwise approximately 20 times. Cut an 18" length of yarn and insert it under all of the strands at the top of the cardboard; pull up **tightly** and tie securely. Leave the yarn ends long enough to attach the tassel. Cut the yarn at the opposite end of the cardboard and then remove it *(Fig. 15a)*. Cut a 6" length of yarn and wrap it **tightly** around the tassel twice, 1" below the top *(Fig. 15b)*; tie securely. Trim the ends.

Fig. 15a

Fig. 15b

Design by Melissa Leapman.

Marvelous Mile-a-Minute

Finished Size: 52" x 66"

MATERIALS

Worsted Weight Yarn:
  Ecru - 25 ounces, (710 grams, 1,715 yards)
  Green - 18 ounces, (510 grams, 1,235 yards)
Crochet hook, size I (5.50 mm) **or** size needed for gauge
Yarn needle

GAUGE: Center = 2³⁄₄"w; 4 rows = 4"
  Each Strip = 5³⁄₄" wide x 66" long

Gauge Swatch: 2³⁄₄"w x 4"h
Work same as Center through Row 4.

STITCH GUIDE

TREBLE CROCHET *(abbreviated tr)*
YO twice, insert hook in st or sp indicated, YO and pull up a loop (4 loops on hook), (YO and draw through 2 loops on hook) 3 times.

SHELL
Tr in st or sp indicated, (ch 1, tr) 5 times in same st or sp.

V-STITCH *(abbreviated V-St)*
(Dc, ch 1, dc) in st or sp indicated.

STRIP (Make 9)
CENTER
With Ecru, ch 10 **loosely**.

Row 1 (Right side)**:** Work Shell in seventh ch from hook, skip next 2 chs, tr in last ch.

Note: Loop a short piece of yarn around any stitch to mark Row 1 as **right** side and bottom edge.

Rows 2-62: Ch 4, turn; skip next 2 ch-1 sps, work Shell in next ch-1 sp, skip next 3 tr, tr in next ch.

Row 63: Ch 6, turn; skip next 2 ch-1 sps, sc in next ch-1 sp, ch 2, skip next 3 tr, tr in next ch; finish off.

Continued on page 39.

EDGING

Rnd 1: With **right** side facing, join Green with slip st in center sc on Row 63; ch 3 **(counts as first dc, now and throughout)**, (4 dc, ch 2, 3 dc) in next sp, 3 dc in end of each row across to last row, (3 dc, ch 2, 4 dc) in last row; dc in free loop of ch at base of Shell **(Fig. 3b, page 1)**, (4 dc, ch 2, 3 dc) in end of first row, 3 dc in end of each row across to last row, (3 dc, ch 2, 4 dc) in last row; join with slip st to first dc, finish off.

Rnd 2: With **right** side facing, join Ecru with slip st in same st as joining; ch 4, dc in same st, skip next 2 dc, work V-St in next dc, † work (V-St, ch 1, V-St) in next corner ch-2 sp, work V-St in center dc of each 3-dc group across to next corner ch-2 sp, work (V-St, ch 1, V-St) in corner ch-2 sp, skip next dc, work V-St in next dc †, (skip next 2 dc, work V-St in next dc) twice, repeat from † to † once; join with slip st to third ch of beginning ch-4, finish off.

Rnd 3: With **right** side facing, join Green with slip st in first ch-1 sp; ch 3, 2 dc in same sp, 3 dc in each ch-1 sp around working (2 dc, ch 3, 2 dc) in each corner ch-1 sp; join with slip st to first dc, finish off.

ASSEMBLY

With Green, working through **inside** loops, and holding bottom edges at same end, whipstitch Strips together beginning in center ch of first corner ch-3 and ending in center ch of next corner ch-3 **(Fig. 5b, page 2)**.

Design by Maggie Weldon.

Naturally Nice

Finished Size: 49" x 62½"

MATERIALS

Worsted Weight Yarn:
   Gold - 21 ounces, (600 grams, 1,440 yards)
   Green - 16 ounces, (450 grams, 1,100 yards)
   Brown - 4 ounces, (110 grams, 275 yards)
Crochet hook, size H (5.00 mm) **or** size needed for gauge

GAUGE SWATCH: 4½" square
Work same as First Square.

STITCH GUIDE

TREBLE CROCHET *(abbreviated tr)*
YO twice, insert hook in sc indicated, YO and pull up a loop (4 loops on hook), (YO and draw through 2 loops on hook) 3 times.

DOUBLE CROCHET CLUSTER
   (abbreviated dc Cluster) (uses one st)
★ YO, insert hook in st indicated, YO and pull up a loop, YO and draw through 2 loops on hook; repeat from ★ 2 times **more**, YO and draw through all 4 loops on hook.

TREBLE CROCHET CLUSTER
   (abbreviated tr Cluster) (uses one ch-3 sp)
★ YO twice, insert hook in ch-3 sp indicated, YO and pull up a loop, (YO and draw through 2 loops on hook) twice; repeat from ★ once **more**, YO and draw through all 3 loops on hook.

FIRST SQUARE

With Brown, ch 3; join with slip st to form a ring.

Rnd 1 (Right side)**:** Ch 1, 6 sc in ring; join with slip st to Front Loop Only of first sc **(Fig. 1, page 1)**.

Note: Loop a short piece of yarn around any stitch to mark Rnd 1 as **right** side.

Rnd 2: Working in Front Loops Only, (dc, slip st) in same st, (slip st, dc, slip st) in next sc and in each sc around pushing dc to **wrong** side; join with slip st to first slip st, finish off.

Rnd 3: With **right** side facing, working behind Rnd 2 and in free loops on Rnd 1 *(Fig. 3a, page 1)*, join Gold with sc in any sc *(see Joining With Sc, page 1)*; sc in same st, 2 sc in next sc and in each sc around; join with slip st to first sc: 12 sc.

Rnd 4: Ch 1, sc in same st, ch 3, (sc in next sc, ch 3) around; join with slip st to first sc.

Rnd 5: Slip st in first ch-3 sp, ch 1, (sc, ch 3, work tr Cluster, ch 3, sc) in same sp and in each ch-3 sp around; join with slip st to first sc, finish off: 12 tr Clusters.

Rnd 6: With **right** side facing, join Green with sc in any tr Cluster; ch 5, sc in next tr Cluster, ch 5, (work dc Cluster, ch 5) twice in next tr Cluster, ★ (sc in next tr Cluster, ch 5) twice, (work dc Cluster, ch 5) twice in next tr Cluster; repeat from ★ 2 times **more**; join with slip st to first sc, finish off.

ADDITIONAL SQUARES

Work same as First Square through Rnd 5: 12 tr Clusters.

Rnd 6 (Joining rnd): Work One or Two Side Joining forming 10 vertical strips of 13 Squares each.

ONE SIDE JOINING

Rnd 6 (Joining rnd): With **right** side facing, join Green with sc in any tr Cluster; ch 5, sc in next tr Cluster, ch 5, ★ (work dc Cluster, ch 5) twice in next tr Cluster, (sc in next tr Cluster, ch 5) twice; repeat from ★ once **more**, work dc Cluster in next tr Cluster, ch 2, holding Squares with **wrong** sides together, slip st in corresponding corner ch-5 sp on **previous Square**, ch 2, work dc Cluster in same st on **new Square**, ch 2, slip st in next ch-5 sp on **previous Square**, ch 2, (sc in next tr Cluster on **new Square**, ch 2, slip st in next ch-5 sp on **previous Square**, ch 2) twice, work dc Cluster in next tr Cluster on **new Square**, ch 2, slip st in next corner ch-5 sp on **previous Square**, ch 2, work dc Cluster in same st on **new Square**, ch 5; join with slip st to first sc, finish off.

TWO SIDE JOINING

Rnd 6 (Joining rnd): With **right** side facing, join Green with sc in any tr Cluster; ch 5, sc in next tr Cluster, ch 5, (work dc Cluster, ch 5) twice in next tr Cluster, (sc in next tr Cluster, ch 5) twice, work dc Cluster in next tr Cluster, ch 2, holding Squares with **wrong** sides together, ★ † slip st in corresponding corner ch-5 sp on **previous Square**, ch 2, work dc Cluster in same st on **new Square** †, ch 2, slip st in next ch-5 sp on **previous Square**, ch 2, (sc in next tr Cluster on **new Square**, ch 2, slip st in next ch-5 sp on **previous Square**, ch 2) twice, work dc Cluster in next tr Cluster on **new Square**, ch 2; repeat from ★ once **more**, then repeat from † to † once, ch 5; join with slip st to first sc, finish off.

EDGING

Rnd 1: With **right** side facing, join Green with sc in any corner ch-5 sp; ch 3, sc in same sp, ch 3, (sc in next sp, ch 3) across to next corner ch-5 sp, ★ (sc, ch 3) twice in corner ch-5 sp, (sc in next sp, ch 3) across to next corner ch-5 sp; repeat from ★ 2 times **more**; join with slip st to first sc: 230 ch-3 sps.

Rnd 2: Ch 1, sc in same st, 3 sc in next ch-3 sp, (sc in next sc, 3 sc in next ch-3 sp) around; join with slip st to first sc, finish off: 920 sc.

Rnd 3: With **wrong** side facing, join Gold with sc in same st as joining; tr in next sc, (sc in next sc pushing tr to **right** side, tr in next sc) around; join with slip st to first sc pushing tr to **right** side, finish off.

Rnd 4: With **right** side facing, join Green with sc in second sc to **left** of joining; ch 1, skip next tr, ★ (sc in next sc, ch 1, skip next tr) across to next corner sc, (sc, ch 1) twice in corner sc, skip next tr; repeat from ★ around; join with slip st to first sc: 928 sts.

Rnd 5: Ch 1, sc in same st, ★ ch 5, skip next 3 sts, sc in next st; repeat from ★ around to last 3 sts, ch 2, skip last 3 sts, dc in first sc to form last ch-5 sp: 232 ch-5 sps.

Rnd 6: Ch 1, (sc, ch 5, sc) in same sp and in each ch-5 sp around; join with slip st to first sc, finish off.

Design by Mary Jane Protus.

Old Fashioned Favorite

Finished Size: 50" x 66"

MATERIALS

Worsted Weight Yarn:
    Off-White - 37 ounces, (1,050 grams, 2,160 yards)
    Lt Rose - 5 ounces, (140 grams, 290 yards)
    Rose - 5 ounces, (140 grams, 290 yards)
    Dk Rose - 5 ounces, (140 grams, 290 yards)
    Lt Blue - 5 ounces, (140 grams, 290 yards)
    Blue - 5 ounces, (140 grams, 290 yards)
    Dk Blue - 5 ounces, (140 grams, 290 yards)
    Green - 5 ounces, (140 grams, 290 yards)
    Peach - 5 ounces, (140 grams, 290 yards)
Crochet hook, size F (3.75 mm) **or** size needed
    for gauge
Yarn needle

GAUGE: Each Motif = 8"
              18 sc and 16 rows = 4"

Gauge Swatch: 4" square
Ch 19 **loosely**.
Row 1: Sc in second ch from hook and in each ch
across: 18 sc.
Rows 2-16: Ch 1, turn; sc in each sc across.
Finish off.

STITCH GUIDE

> **TREBLE CROCHET** *(abbreviated tr)*
> YO twice, insert hook in sc indicated, YO and pull
> up a loop (4 loops on hook), (YO and draw through
> 2 loops on hook) 3 times.

MOTIF (Make 48)
CENTER
Rnd 1 (Right side)**:** With Off-White, ch 2, 8 sc in second
ch from hook; join with slip st to first sc.

Note: Loop a short piece of yarn around any stitch to
mark Rnd 1 as **right** side.

Rnd 2: Ch 1, 2 sc in same st and in each sc around;
join with slip st to first sc changing to Lt Rose *(Fig. 2b,
page 1)*: 16 sc.

PETALS
Ch 11 **loosely**.

Row 1: Hdc in third ch from hook **(2 skipped chs
count as first hdc)** and in next ch, sc in next 4 chs,
slip st in last 3 chs and in **same** sc as joining on Rnd 2 of
Center: 11 sts.

Note: Work in Back Loops Only throughout Petals
(Fig. 1, page 1).

Row 2: Turn; skip first slip st, slip st in next 3 slip sts, sc
in next 4 sc, hdc in last 3 hdc: 10 sts.

Row 3: Ch 2 **(counts as first hdc, now and
throughout)**, turn; hdc in next 2 hdc, sc in next 4
sc, slip st in last 3 slip sts and in **same** sc on Rnd 2 of
Center: 11 sts.

Row 4: Turn; skip first slip st, slip st in next 3 slip sts, sc
in next 4 sc, hdc in last 3 hdc: 10 sts.

Row 5: Ch 2, turn; hdc in next 2 hdc, sc in next 4
sc, slip st in last 3 slip sts and in **next** sc on Rnd 2 of
Center: 11 sts.

Row 6: Turn; skip first slip st, slip st in next 3 slip sts, sc
in next 4 sc, hdc in last 3 hdc: 10 sts.

Row 7: Ch 2, turn; hdc in next 2 hdc, sc in next 4
sc, slip st in last 3 slip sts and in **same** sc on Rnd 2 of
Center: 11 sts.

Row 8: Turn; skip first slip st, slip st in next 3 slip sts, sc in next 4 sc, hdc in last 3 hdc changing to Blue in last hdc *(Fig. 2a, page 1)*: 10 sts.

Rows 9-16: Repeat Rows 5-8 twice changing to Green in last hdc on Row 16.

Rows 17-24: Repeat Rows 5-8 twice changing to Dk Rose in last hdc on Row 24.

Rows 25-32: Repeat Rows 5-8 twice changing to Lt Blue in last hdc on Row 32.

Rows 33-40: Repeat Rows 5-8 twice changing to Rose in last hdc on Row 40.

Rows 41-48: Repeat Rows 5-8 twice changing to Peach in last hdc on Row 48.

Rows 49-56: Repeat Rows 5-8 twice changing to Dk Blue in last hdc on Row 56.

Rows 57-64: Repeat Rows 5-8 twice; do **not** change colors at the end of Row 64.

Row 65 (Joining row)**:** Turn; with **right** side together and working in Back Loop Only of each st on Row 64 **and** in free loops of beginning ch *(Fig. 3b, page 1)*, slip st in each st across; finish off.

BORDER

Rnd 1: With **right** side facing and working in end of rows, join Off-White with sc in last row *(see Joining With Sc, page 1)*; 2 sc in same row, skip next row, (3 sc in next row, skip next row) around; join with slip st to first sc: 96 sc.

Rnd 2: Ch 4 **(counts as first tr)**, (2 tr, ch 2, 3 tr) in same st, ★ † ch 1, skip next 3 sc, 2 dc in next sc, ch 1, skip next 3 sc, 2 hdc in next sc, ch 1, skip next 3 sc, 2 sc in next sc, ch 1, skip next 3 sc, 2 hdc in next sc, ch 1, skip next 3 sc, 2 dc in next sc, ch 1, skip next 3 sc †, (3 tr, ch 2, 3 tr) in next sc; repeat from ★ 2 times **more**, then repeat from † to † once; join with slip st to first tr: 64 sts and 28 sps.

Rnd 3: Ch 1, sc in same st and in next 2 tr, 3 sc in next corner ch-2 sp, sc in each st and in each ch-1 sp around working 3 sc in each corner ch-2 sp; join with slip st to first sc: 100 sc.

Rnd 4: Ch 1, sc in same st and in each sc around working 3 sc in center sc of each corner 3-sc group; join with slip st to first sc, finish off: 108 sc.

ASSEMBLY

With Off-White and working in **inside** loops, whipstitch Motifs together forming 6 vertical strips of 8 Motifs each *(Fig. 5b, page 2)*, beginning in center sc of first corner 3-sc group and ending in center sc of next corner 3-sc group; then whipstitch strips together in same manner.

EDGING

Rnd 1: With **right** side facing, join Off-White with sc in center sc of top right corner 3-sc group; 2 sc in same st, † work 183 sc evenly spaced across to center sc of next corner 3-sc group, 3 sc in center sc, work 243 sc evenly spaced across to center sc of next corner 3-sc group †, 3 sc in center sc, repeat from † to † once; join with slip st to first sc: 864 sc.

Rnd 2: Ch 2, ★ † sc in next sc, hdc in next sc, dc in next sc, 3 tr in next sc, dc in next sc †, hdc in next sc; repeat from ★ around to last 5 sc, then repeat from † to † once; join with slip st to first hdc, finish off.

Design by Sarah Anne Phillips.

# Pretty in Peach

Finished Size: 48" x 64"

MATERIALS
Worsted Weight Yarn:
    44 ounces, (1,250 grams, 2,565 yards)
    Crochet hook, size K (6.50 mm) **or** size needed
      for gauge

GAUGE: 12 dc and 7 rows = 4"

Gauge Swatch: 4" square
Ch 14 **loosely**.
Row 1: Dc in fourth ch from hook **(3 skipped chs count as first dc)** and in each ch across: 12 dc.
Rows 2-7: Ch 3 **(counts as first dc)**, turn; dc in next dc and in each dc across.
Finish off.

STITCH GUIDE

> **TREBLE CROCHET** *(abbreviated tr)*
> YO twice, insert hook in sp indicated, YO and pull up a loop (4 loops on hook), (YO and draw through 2 loops on hook) 3 times.

AFGHAN BODY
Ch 146 **loosely**.

Row 1: Dc in fourth ch from hook **(3 skipped chs count as first dc)** and in next 3 chs, ch 2, ★ skip next 2 chs, dc in next 10 chs, ch 2; repeat from ★ across to last 7 chs, skip next 2 chs, dc in last 5 chs: 120 dc and 12 ch-2 sps.

Row 2 (Right side)**:** Ch 3 **(counts as first dc, now and throughout)**, turn; dc in next 2 dc, (tr, 4 dc, tr) in next ch-2 sp, ★ skip next 2 dc, dc in next 6 dc, (tr, 4 dc, tr) in next ch-2 sp; repeat from ★ across to last 5 dc, skip next 2 dc, dc in last 3 dc: 144 sts.

Note: Loop a short piece of yarn around any stitch to mark Row 2 as **right** side.

Row 3: Ch 3, turn; dc in next dc, skip next dc, 2 dc in sp **before** next tr, skip next 2 sts, dc in next dc, ch 2, dc in next dc, skip next 2 sts, 2 dc in sp **before** next dc, ★ skip next dc, dc in next 4 dc, skip next dc, 2 dc in sp **before** next tr, skip next 2 sts, dc in next dc, ch 2, dc in next dc, skip next 2 sts, 2 dc in sp **before** next dc; repeat from ★ across to last 3 dc, skip next dc, dc in last 2 dc: 120 dc and 12 ch-2 sps.

Row 4: Ch 3, turn; dc in next 2 dc, (tr, 4 dc, tr) in next ch-2 sp, ★ skip next 2 dc, dc in next 6 dc, (tr, 4 dc, tr) in next ch-2 sp; repeat from ★ across to last 5 dc, skip next 2 dc, dc in last 3 dc: 144 sts.

Rows 5-110: Repeat Rows 3 and 4, 53 times.

Row 111: Ch 3, turn; dc in next 2 dc, hdc in next tr, sc in next 4 dc, hdc in next tr, ★ dc in next 6 dc, hdc in next tr, sc in next 4 dc, hdc in next tr; repeat from ★ across to last 3 dc, dc in last 3 dc; do **not** finish off: 144 sts.

EDGING
TOP
Row 1: Ch 5, turn; skip next dc, sc in next dc, ★ ch 5, skip next 2 sts, sc in next st; repeat from ★ across to last 3 dc, ch 2, skip next 2 dc, dc in last dc to form last ch-5 sp: 48 ch-5 sps.

Row 2: Ch 1, turn; sc in same sp, (ch 5, sc in next ch-5 sp) across; finish off.

BOTTOM
Row 1: With **right** side facing and working in free loops of beginning ch *(Fig. 3b, page 1)*, join yarn with slip st in first ch; ch 5, skip next ch, sc in next ch, ★ ch 5, skip next 2 chs, sc in next ch; repeat from ★ across to last 3 chs, ch 2, skip next 2 chs, dc in last ch to form last ch-5 sp: 48 ch-5 sps.

Row 2: Ch 1, turn; sc in same sp, (ch 5, sc in next ch-5 sp) across; finish off.

Holding 6 strands of yarn together, each 11" long, add fringe in each sp across short edges of Afghan *(Figs. 6a & b, page 2)*.

Design by Mary Lamb Becker.

Quick & Easy Choices

LONG STITCH AFGHAN
Finished Size: 48" x 62"

MATERIALS
Worsted Weight Yarn:
Copper - 21 ounces, (600 grams, 1,440 yards)
Green - 21 ounces, (600 grams, 1,440 yards)
Burgundy - 20 ounces, (570 grams, 1,370 yards)
Gold - 20 ounces, (570 grams, 1,370 yards)
Crochet hook, size N (9.00 mm) **or** size needed for gauge

Note: Afghan is worked holding two strands of yarn together.

GAUGE: In pattern, 9 sc = 4"; 16 rows = 5"

Gauge Swatch: 4"w x 5"h
Ch 10 **loosely**.
Work same as Afghan Body for 16 rows.
Finish off.

STITCH GUIDE

LONG SINGLE CROCHET *(abbreviated LSC)*
Working **around** next sc, insert hook in st indicated *(Fig. 16a)*, YO and pull up a loop even with loop on hook, YO and draw through both loops on hook *(Fig. 16b)* **(counts as one sc)**.

Fig. 16a   **Fig. 16b**

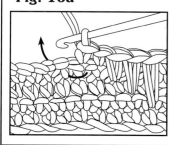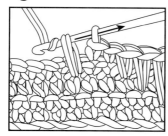

AFGHAN BODY
With Copper, ch 108 **loosely**.

Row 1 (Right side)**:** Sc in second ch from hook and in each ch across: 107 sc.

Rows 2-4: Ch 1, turn; sc in each sc across changing to Green in last sc made on Row 4 *(Fig. 2a, page 1)*.

Row 5: Ch 1, turn; sc in first 2 sc, ★ work LSC in sc one row **below** next sc *(Figs. 16a & b)*, work LSC in sc 2 rows **below** next sc, work LSC in sc 3 rows **below** next sc, work LSC in sc 2 rows **below** next sc, work LSC in sc one row **below** next sc, sc in next 2 sc; repeat from ★ across.

Rows 6-8: Ch 1, turn; sc in each sc across changing to Burgundy in last sc on Row 8.

Rows 9-12: Repeat Rows 5-8 changing to Gold in last sc on Row 12.

Rows 13-16: Repeat Rows 5-8 changing to Copper in last sc on Row 16.

Rows 17-20: Repeat Rows 5-8 changing to Green in last sc on Row 20.

Rows 21-196: Repeat Rows 5-20, 11 times.

EDGING
Ch 1, turn; sc evenly around entire Afghan Body working 3 sc in each corner; join with slip st to first sc, finish off.

Design by Carole Prior.

SLANT STITCH AFGHAN
Finished Size: 48" x 62"

MATERIALS
Worsted Weight Yarn:
61 ounces, (1,730 grams, 4,185 yards)
Crochet hook, size N (9.00 mm) **or** size needed for gauge

Note: Each row is worked across length of Afghan holding two strands of yarn together.

GAUGE: In pattern, 8 sts = 3"; 4 rows = 3½"

Gauge Swatch: 3¾"w x 3½"h
Ch 12 **loosely**.
Work same as Afghan Body for 4 rows.
Finish off.

Continued on page 45.

STITCH GUIDE

SLANT STITCH (abbreviated Slant St)

YO, working **around** last 3-dc group made, insert hook in same st as first dc of 3-dc group, YO and pull up a loop even with loop on hook *(Fig. 17)*, (YO and draw through 2 loops on hook) twice.

Fig. 17

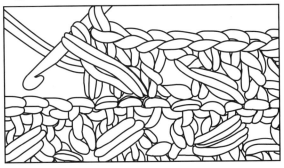

REVERSE HALF DOUBLE CROCHET
(abbreviated reverse hdc)

Working from **left** to **right**, YO, insert hook in st indicated to right of hook *(Fig. 18a)*, YO and draw through, under and to left of loops on hook (3 loops on hook) *(Fig. 18b)*, YO and draw through all 3 loops on hook *(Fig. 18c)* **(reverse hdc made, Fig. 18d)**.

Fig. 18a

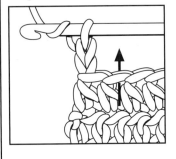

Fig. 18b

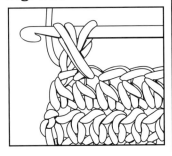

Fig. 18c

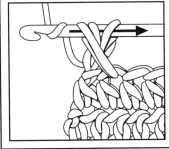

Fig. 18d

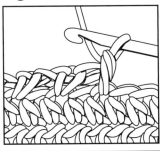

AFGHAN BODY

Ch 160 **loosely**.

Row 1 (Right side)**:** Dc in fourth ch from hook **(3 skipped chs count as first dc)** and in next 2 chs, work Slant St *(Fig. 17)*, ★ skip next ch, dc in next 3 chs, work Slant St; repeat from ★ across to last 2 chs, skip next ch, dc in last ch: 39 Slant Sts.

Rows 2-53: Ch 3 **(counts as first dc)**, turn; dc in next 3 sts, work Slant St, ★ skip next dc, dc in next 3 sts, work Slant St; repeat from ★ across to last 2 dc, skip next dc, dc in last dc; do **not** finish off.

EDGING

Rnd 1: Ch 1, do **not** turn; 2 sc in end of each row across; working in free loops of beginning ch *(Fig. 3b, page 1)*, sc in each ch across; 2 sc in end of each row across; sc in each st across Row 53; join with slip st to first sc: 528 sc.

Rnd 2: Ch 1, hdc in same st, ch 1; working from **left** to **right**, skip next sc, ★ work reverse hdc in next sc *(Figs. 18a-d)*, ch 1, skip next sc; repeat from ★ around; join with slip st to first hdc, finish off.

Design by Carole Prior.

 Romantic Ripple

Finished Size: 49" x 65½"

MATERIALS

Worsted Weight Yarn:
Taupe - 20 ounces, (570 grams, 1,315 yards)
Lt Rose - 15 ounces, (430 grams, 985 yards)
Rose - 15 ounces, (430 grams, 985 yards)
Crochet hook, size I (5.50 mm) **or** size needed
for gauge

GAUGE: In pattern, one repeat = 3¼"; 6 rows = 4"

Gauge Swatch: 6½"w x 5"h
Ch 31 **loosely**.
Work same as Afghan for 6 rows.

STITCH GUIDE

POPCORN
4 Dc in st indicated, drop loop from hook, insert
hook in first dc of 4-dc group, hook dropped loop
and draw through.

DECREASE (uses next 2 dc)
★ YO, insert hook in **next** dc, YO and pull up a
loop, YO and draw through 2 loops on hook; repeat
from ★ once **more**, YO and draw through all 3 loops
on hook **(counts as one dc)**.

AFGHAN

With Taupe, ch 213 **loosely**.

Row 1 (Right side)**:** 2 Dc in fourth ch from hook
(3 skipped chs count as first dc), dc in next 3 chs,
skip next ch, work Popcorn in next ch, skip next 2 chs,
work Popcorn in next ch, skip next ch, dc in next 3 chs,
★ (dc, ch 1, dc) in next 2 chs, dc in next 3 chs, skip
next ch, work Popcorn in next ch, skip next 2 chs, work
Popcorn in next ch, skip next ch, dc in next 3 chs; repeat
from ★ across to last ch, 3 dc in last ch: 152 dc and
30 Popcorns.

Note: Loop a short piece of yarn around any stitch to
mark Row 1 as **right** side.

Row 2: Ch 3 **(counts as first dc, now and
throughout)**, turn; 2 dc in same st, dc in next 3 dc,
decrease, skip next 2 Popcorns, decrease, ★ dc in next
2 dc and in next ch-1 sp, (dc, ch 1, dc) in next 2 dc, dc
in next ch-1 sp and in next 2 dc, decrease, skip next
2 Popcorns, decrease; repeat from ★ across to last 4 dc,
dc in next 3 dc, 3 dc in last dc; finish off: 182 dc.

Row 3: With **right** side facing, join Lt Rose with slip
st in first dc; ch 3, 2 dc in same st, dc in next 3 dc, skip
next dc, work Popcorn in next dc, skip next 2 dc, work
Popcorn in next dc, ★ skip next dc, dc in next 2 dc and
in next ch-1 sp, (dc, ch 1, dc) in next 2 dc, dc in next
ch-1 sp and in next 2 dc, skip next dc, work Popcorn in
next dc, skip next 2 dc, work Popcorn in next dc; repeat
from ★ across to last 5 dc, skip next dc, dc in next 3 dc,
3 dc in last dc.

Row 4: Ch 3, turn; 2 dc in same st, dc in next 3 dc,
decrease, skip next 2 Popcorns, decrease, ★ dc in next
2 dc and in next ch-1 sp, (dc, ch 1, dc) in next 2 dc, dc
in next ch-1 sp and in next 2 dc, decrease, skip next
2 Popcorns, decrease; repeat from ★ across to last 4 dc,
dc in next 3 dc, 3 dc in last dc; finish off.

Row 5: With **right** side facing, join Rose with slip st
in first dc; ch 3, 2 dc in same st, dc in next 3 dc, skip
next dc, work Popcorn in next dc, skip next 2 dc, work
Popcorn in next dc, ★ skip next dc, dc in next 2 dc and
in next ch-1 sp, (dc, ch 1, dc) in next 2 dc, dc in next
ch-1 sp and in next 2 dc, skip next dc, work Popcorn in
next dc, skip next 2 dc, work Popcorn in next dc; repeat
from ★ across to last 5 dc, skip next dc, dc in next 3 dc,
3 dc in last dc.

Row 6: Ch 3, turn; 2 dc in same st, dc in next 3 dc,
decrease, skip next 2 Popcorns, decrease, ★ dc in next
2 dc and in next ch-1 sp, (dc, ch 1, dc) in next 2 dc, dc
in next ch-1 sp and in next 2 dc, decrease, skip next
2 Popcorns, decrease; repeat from ★ across to last 4 dc,
dc in next 3 dc, 3 dc in last dc; finish off.

Row 7: With **right** side facing, join Taupe with slip st
in first dc; ch 3, 2 dc in same st, dc in next 3 dc, skip
next dc, work Popcorn in next dc, skip next 2 dc, work
Popcorn in next dc, ★ skip next dc, dc in next 2 dc and
in next ch-1 sp, (dc, ch 1, dc) in next 2 dc, dc in next
ch-1 sp and in next 2 dc, skip next dc, work Popcorn in
next dc, skip next 2 dc, work Popcorn in next dc; repeat
from ★ across to last 5 dc, skip next dc, dc in next 3 dc,
3 dc in last dc.

Row 8: Ch 3, turn; 2 dc in same st, dc in next 3 dc,
decrease, skip next 2 Popcorns, decrease, ★ dc in next
2 dc and in next ch-1 sp, (dc, ch 1, dc) in next 2 dc, dc
in next ch-1 sp and in next 2 dc, decrease, skip next
2 Popcorns, decrease; repeat from ★ across to last 4 dc,
dc in next 3 dc, 3 dc in last dc; finish off.

Rows 9-98: Repeat Rows 3-8, 15 times.

Holding 12 strands of Taupe yarn together, each
17" long, add fringe in each point across short edges of
Afghan *(Figs. 6a & b, page 2)*.

Design by Carole Prior.

Sweet Dreams

Finished Size: 34" x 45"

MATERIALS
Worsted Weight Brushed Acrylic Yarn:
- **Solid version**
    - 21 ounces, (600 grams, 1,620 yards)
- **Striped version**
    - White - 10 ounces, (280 grams, 770 yards)
    - Yellow - 5½ ounces, (160 grams, 425 yards)
    - Blue - 5½ ounces, (160 grams, 425 yards)
- Crochet hook, size H (5.00 mm) **or** size needed for gauge

GAUGE: In pattern, 3 repeats and 9 rows = 3"

Gauge Swatch: 4"w x 3"h
Ch 16 **loosely.**
Work same as Afghan Body for 9 rows.
Finish off.

STITCH GUIDE

> **PUFF STITCH** *(abbreviated Puff St)*
> ★ YO, insert hook in ch-1 sp indicated, YO and pull up a loop even with loop on hook; repeat from ★ 2 times **more**, YO and draw through all 7 loops on hook.

SOLID AFGHAN
AFGHAN BODY
Ch 128 **loosely.**

Row 1 (Right side)**:** Sc in second ch from hook and in each ch across: 127 sc.

Row 2: Ch 1, turn; sc in first sc, ★ ch 1, skip next sc, sc in next sc; repeat from ★ across: 64 sc and 63 ch-1 sps.

Row 3: Ch 3 **(counts as first dc)**, turn; work Puff St in first ch-1 sp, ★ ch 3, slip st in next ch-1 sp, ch 3, work Puff St in next ch-1 sp; repeat from ★ across to last sc, ch 1, dc in last sc: 32 Puff Sts and 62 ch-3 sps.

Row 4: Ch 1, turn; sc in first dc and in next Puff St, ★ sc in next ch-3 sp, ch 1, sc in next ch-3 sp and in next Puff St; repeat from ★ across to last dc, sc in last dc: 127 sts.

Row 5: Ch 1, turn; sc in first sc, ★ ch 1, skip next st, sc in next sc; repeat from ★ across: 64 sc and 63 ch-1 sps.

Rows 6-122: Repeat Rows 3-5, 39 times; do **not** finish off.

EDGING
Rnd 1: Ch 1, turn; sc in first sc, ch 3, (skip next 3 sts, sc in next st, ch 3) twice, (skip next 2 sts, sc in next st, ch 3) across to last 4 sts, skip next 3 sts, (sc, ch 3) twice in last sc; † working in end of rows, skip first row, [(sc in next row, ch 3) twice, skip next row] 3 times, [(sc in next row, ch 3) twice, skip next 2 rows, (sc in next row, ch 3) twice, skip next row] across †; working in free loops of beginning ch *(Fig. 3b, page 1)*, (sc, ch 3) twice in first ch, (skip next 3 chs, sc in next ch, ch 3) twice, (skip next 2 chs, sc in next ch, ch 3) across to last 4 chs, skip next 3 chs, (sc, ch 3) twice in last ch; repeat from † to † once; sc in same st as first sc, ch 3; join with slip st to first sc: 228 ch-3 sps.

Rnd 2: Slip st in first ch-3 sp, ch 3, work Puff St in next ch-3 sp, ch 3, ★ slip st in next ch-3 sp, ch 3, work Puff St in next ch-3 sp, ch 3; repeat from ★ around; join with slip st to first slip st, finish off.

STRIPED AFGHAN
AFGHAN BODY
With White, ch 128 **loosely.**

Row 1 (Right side)**:** Sc in second ch from hook and in each ch across: 127 sc.

Note: Loop a short piece of yarn around any stitch to mark Row 1 as **right** side.

Row 2: Ch 1, turn; sc in first sc, ★ ch 1, skip next st, sc in next sc; repeat from ★ across changing to Yellow in last sc *(Fig. 2a, page 1)*: 64 sc and 63 ch-1 sps.

Row 3: Ch 3 **(counts as first dc, now and throughout)**, turn; work Puff St in first ch-1 sp, ★ ch 3, slip st in next ch-1 sp, ch 3, work Puff St in next ch-1 sp; repeat from ★ across to last sc, ch 1, dc in last sc; finish off: 32 Puff Sts and 62 ch-3 sps.

Row 4: With **right** side facing, join White with slip st in first dc; ch 1, sc in same st and in next Puff St, ★ sc in next ch-3 sp, ch 1, sc in next ch-3 sp and in next Puff St; repeat from ★ across to last dc, sc in last dc: 127 sts.

Row 5: Ch 1, turn; sc in first sc, ★ ch 1, skip next st, sc in next sc; repeat from ★ across changing to Blue in last sc: 64 sc and 63 ch-1 sps.

Row 6: Ch 3, turn; work Puff St in first ch-1 sp, ★ ch 3, slip st in next ch-1 sp, ch 3, work Puff St in next ch-1 sp; repeat from ★ across to last sc, ch 1, dc in last sc; finish off: 32 Puff Sts and 62 ch-3 sps.

Row 7: With **right** side facing, join White with slip st in first dc; ch 1, sc in same st and in next Puff St, ★ sc in next ch-3 sp, ch 1, sc in next ch-3 sp and in next Puff St; repeat from ★ across to last dc, sc in last dc: 127 sts.

Rows 8-121: Repeat Rows 2-7, 19 times.

Row 122: Ch 1, turn; sc in first sc, ★ ch 1, skip next st, sc in next sc; repeat from ★ across; do **not** finish off: 64 sc and 63 ch-1 sps.

EDGING
Work same as Solid Afghan.

Design by Jennine Korejko.

Touch of Spring

Finished Size: 53½" x 64"

MATERIALS
Worsted Weight Yarn:
  Ecru - 38 ounces, (1,080 grams, 2,605 yards)
  Blue - 19 ounces, (540 grams, 1,305 yards)
  Mauve - 2 ounces, (60 grams, 140 yards)
  Violet - 2 ounces, (60 grams, 140 yards)
  Green - 1 ounce, (30 grams, 70 yards)
  Yellow - 1 ounce, (30 grams, 70 yards)
Crochet hooks, sizes H (5.00 mm) **and** I (5.50 mm)
  or sizes needed for gauge
Yarn needle

GAUGE: Each Square = 10½"
  Each Flower = 5½" long x ¾" wide
  (before gathering)

Gauge Swatch: 2" diameter
Work same as Square Rnds 1-3.

STITCH GUIDE

TREBLE CROCHET *(abbreviated tr)*
YO twice, insert hook in st or sp indicated, YO and pull up a loop (4 loops on hook), (YO and draw through 2 loops on hook) 3 times.

POPCORN
3 Sc in st or sp indicated, drop loop from hook, insert hook in first sc of 3-sc group, hook dropped loop and draw through.

SQUARE (Make 30)
Rnd 1 (Right side)**:** With Ecru and large size hook, ch 2, 6 sc in second ch from hook; join with slip st to first sc.

Note: Loop a short piece of yarn around any stitch to mark Rnd 1 as **right** side.

Rnd 2: Ch 1, 2 sc in same st and in each sc around; join with slip st to first sc: 12 sc.

Rnd 3: Ch 5, (dc, hdc) in next sc, hdc in next sc, ★ (hdc, dc) in next sc, ch 2, (dc, hdc) in next sc, hdc in next sc; repeat from ★ 2 times **more**, hdc in same st as beginning ch-5; join with slip st to third ch of beginning ch-5: 20 sts and 4 ch-2 sps.

Rnd 4: Slip st in first ch-2 sp, ch 3 **(counts as first dc, now and throughout)**, turn; dc in same sp and in each st across to next corner ch-2 sp, ★ (2 dc, ch 1, 2 dc) in corner ch-2 sp, dc in each st across to next corner ch-2 sp; repeat from ★ 2 times **more**, 2 dc in same sp as first dc, ch 1; join with slip st to first dc; do **not** finish off: 36 dc.

Continued on page 49.

Rnd 5: Turn; slip st in first ch-1 sp, ch 4, 2 dc in same sp, dc in each dc across to next corner ch-1 sp, ★ (2 dc, ch 1, 2 dc) in corner ch-1 sp, dc in each dc across to next corner ch-1 sp; repeat from ★ 2 times **more**, dc in same sp as beginning ch-4; join with slip st to third ch of beginning ch-4: 52 sts and 4 ch-1 sps.

Rnd 6: Slip st in next ch, ch 3, turn; working in Front Loops Only *(Fig. 1, page 1)*, dc in same st and in each dc across to next corner ch-1, ★ (2 dc, ch 1, 2 dc) in corner ch-1, dc in each dc across to next corner ch-1; repeat from ★ 2 times **more**, 2 dc in same st as first dc, ch 1; join with slip st to first dc: 68 dc.

Rnd 7: Turn; slip st in first ch-1 sp, ch 5, 2 tr in same sp, working in both loops, dc in each dc across to next corner ch-1 sp, ★ (2 tr, ch 1, 2 tr) in corner ch-1 sp, dc in each dc across to next corner ch-1 sp; repeat from ★ 2 times **more**, tr in same sp as beginning ch-5; join with slip st to fourth ch of beginning ch-5: 84 sts and 4 ch-1 sps.

Rnd 8: Slip st in first ch-1 sp, ch 4, turn; tr in same sp, dc in each st across to next corner ch-1 sp, ★ (2 tr, ch 1, 2 tr) in corner ch-1 sp, dc in each st across to next corner ch-1 sp; repeat from ★ 2 times **more**, 2 tr in same sp as beginning ch-4, ch 1; join with slip st to top of beginning ch-4: 100 sts and 4 ch-1 sps.

Rnd 9: Turn; slip st in first ch-1 sp, ch 5, 2 tr in same sp, dc in each st across to next corner ch-1 sp, ★ (2 tr, ch 1, 2 tr) in corner ch-1 sp, dc in each st across to next corner ch-1 sp; repeat from ★ 2 times **more**, tr in same sp as beginning ch-5; join with slip st to fourth ch of beginning ch-5, finish off: 116 sts and 4 ch-1 sps.

Rnd 10: With **right** side facing, join Blue with slip st in any corner ch-1 sp; ch 1, work (Popcorn, ch 2, Popcorn) in same sp, sc in next 2 tr, (work Popcorn in next dc, sc in next 2 sts) across to next corner ch-1 sp, ★ work (Popcorn, ch 2, Popcorn) in corner ch-1 sp, sc in next 2 tr, (work Popcorn in next dc, sc in next 2 sts) across to next corner ch-1 sp; repeat from ★ 2 times **more**; join with slip st to top of first Popcorn, finish off: 44 Popcorns.

Rnd 11: With **right** side facing, join Ecru with sc in first ch of any corner ch-2 *(see Joining With Sc, page 1)*; ch 2, sc in next ch and in each st across to next corner ch-2, ★ sc in next ch, ch 2, sc in next ch and in each st across to next corner ch-2; repeat from ★ 2 times **more**; join with slip st to first sc, finish off: 132 sc.

FLOWER

Note: Make 30 **each** of Blue, Mauve and Violet.

With color indicated and small size hook, ch 21 **loosely**; sc in second ch from hook, (hdc, dc) in next ch, (dc, hdc) in next ch, sc in next ch, slip st in next ch, ★ sc in next ch, (hdc, dc) in next ch, (dc, hdc) in next ch, sc in next ch, slip st in next ch; repeat from ★ 2 times **more**; finish off leaving a long end for sewing.

Thread needle with end and weave through free loops of beginning ch *(Fig. 3b, page 1)*; gather tightly and secure.

FLOWER CENTER (Make 90)

With Yellow and small size hook, ch 2, 4 sc in second ch from hook; join with slip st to first sc, finish off leaving a long end for sewing.

Sew Center to Flower.

LEAF (Make 30)

With Green and small size hook, ★ ch 6 **loosely**, sc in second ch from hook and in next 3 chs, slip st in last ch; repeat from ★ 2 times **more**; finish off leaving a long end for sewing.

Sew Leaves to back of Mauve Flowers.

Using photo as a guide, page 31, sew Flowers and Leaves to center of each Square.

ASSEMBLY

With Ecru and working through **inside** loops, whipstitch Squares together forming 5 vertical strips of 6 Squares each *(Fig. 5b, page 2)*, beginning in second ch of first corner ch-2 and ending in first ch of next corner ch-2; then whipstitch strips together in same manner.

EDGING

With **right** side facing, large size hook, and working in Back Loops Only, join Ecru with slip st in first ch of any corner ch-2; ch 3, dc in same st, ★ † ch 2, 2 dc in next ch, dc in next 33 sc, (dc in next ch, tr in next joining, dc in next ch and in next 33 sc) across to next corner ch-2 †, 2 dc in next ch; repeat from ★ 2 times **more**, then repeat from † to † once; join with slip st to first dc, finish off.

Design by Nancy Fuller.

Understated Elegance

Finished Size: 46" x 56"

MATERIALS
Worsted Weight Yarn:
   66 ounces, (1,870 grams, 3,850 yards)
   Crochet hook, size G (4.00 mm) **or** size needed
    for gauge

GAUGE: In pattern, 16 sts and 12 rows = 4"

Gauge Swatch: 4" square
Ch 18 **loosely**.
Row 1: Dc in fourth ch from hook **(3 skipped chs count as first dc)** and in each ch across: 16 dc.
Row 2: Ch 1, turn; sc in each dc across.
Row 3: Ch 3 **(counts as first dc)**, turn; dc in next sc and in each sc across.
Rows 4-12: Repeat Rows 2 and 3, 4 times; then repeat Row 2 once **more**.
Finish off.

STITCH GUIDE

POPCORN
5 Dc in next sc, drop loop from hook, insert hook in first dc of 5-dc group, hook dropped loop and draw through, ch 1 to close.

AFGHAN BODY
Ch 181 **loosely**.

Row 1 (Right side)**:** Dc in fourth ch from hook **(3 skipped chs count as first dc)** and in each ch across: 179 dc.

Note: Loop a short piece of yarn around any stitch to mark Row 1 as **right** side.

Row 2: Ch 1, turn; sc in each dc across.

Row 3: Ch 3 **(counts as first dc, now and throughout)**, turn; dc in next 11 sc, work Popcorn, (dc in next 21 sc, work Popcorn) across to last 12 sc, dc in last 12 sc: 8 Popcorns.

Row 4: Ch 1, turn; sc in each st across: 179 sc.

Row 5: Ch 3, turn; dc in next 9 sc, work Popcorn, dc in next 3 sc, work Popcorn, ★ dc in next 17 sc, work Popcorn, dc in next 3 sc, work Popcorn; repeat from ★ across to last 10 sc, dc in last 10 sc: 16 Popcorns.

Row 6: Ch 1, turn; sc in each st across: 179 sc.

Row 7: Ch 3, turn; (dc in next 7 sc, work Popcorn) twice, ★ dc in next 13 sc, work Popcorn, dc in next 7 sc, work Popcorn; repeat from ★ across to last 8 sc, dc in last 8 sc: 16 Popcorns.

Row 8: Ch 1, turn; sc in each st across: 179 sc.

Row 9: Ch 3, turn; dc in next 5 sc, work Popcorn, dc in next 5 sc, ch 1, skip next sc, dc in next 5 sc, work Popcorn, ★ dc in next 9 sc, work Popcorn, dc in next 5 sc, ch 1, skip next sc, dc in next 5 sc, work Popcorn; repeat from ★ across to last 6 sc, dc in last 6 sc: 16 Popcorns and 8 ch-1 sps.

Row 10: Ch 1, turn; sc in each st and in each ch-1 sp across: 179 sc.

Row 11: Ch 3, turn; dc in next 3 sc, work Popcorn, dc in next 6 sc, ch 1, skip next sc, dc in next sc, ch 1, skip next sc, dc in next 6 sc, work Popcorn, ★ dc in next 5 sc, work Popcorn, dc in next 6 sc, ch 1, skip next sc, dc in next sc, ch 1, skip next sc, dc in next 6 sc, work Popcorn; repeat from ★ across to last 4 sc, dc in last 4 sc: 16 Popcorns and 16 ch-1 sps.

Row 12: Ch 1, turn; sc in each st and in each ch-1 sp across: 179 sc.

Rows 13 and 14: Repeat Rows 9 and 10.

Rows 15 and 16: Repeat Rows 7 and 8.

Rows 17 and 18: Repeat Rows 5 and 6.

Rows 19 and 20: Repeat Rows 3 and 4.

Row 21: Ch 3, turn; dc in next sc and in each sc across.

Row 22: Ch 1, turn; sc in each dc across.

Row 23: Ch 3, turn; dc in next sc, ch 1, ★ skip next sc, dc in next sc, ch 1; repeat from ★ across to last 3 sc, skip next sc, dc in last 2 sc: 91 dc and 88 ch-1 sps.

Row 24: Ch 1, turn; sc in each dc and in each ch-1 sp across: 179 sc.

Row 25: Ch 3, turn; dc in next sc and in each sc across.

Rows 26-165: Repeat Rows 2-25, 5 times; then repeat Rows 2-21 once **more**; do **not** finish off.

EDGING
Rnd 1: Ch 1, do **not** turn; work 221 sc evenly spaced across end of rows; working in free loops of beginning ch *(Fig. 3b, page 1)*, 3 sc in first ch, sc in each ch across to ch at base of last dc, 3 sc in ch at base of last dc; work 221 sc evenly spaced across end of rows; working in sts across Row 165, 3 sc in first dc, sc in each dc across to last dc, 3 sc in last dc; join with slip st to first sc: 808 sc.

Rnd 2: Slip st in next sc, ch 4, skip next sc, dc in next sc, ★ (ch 1, skip next sc, dc in next sc) across to center sc of next corner 3-sc group, ch 3, skip center sc, dc in next sc; repeat from ★ around to last st, ch 1, skip last st; join with slip st to third ch of beginning ch-4, finish off.

Holding 6 strands of yarn together, each 17" long, add fringe evenly spaced across short edges of Afghan *(Figs. 6a & b, page 2)*.

Design by Shobha Govindan.

Very Victorian

Finished Size: 50" x 71"

MATERIALS
Worsted Weight Yarn:
39 ounces, (1,110 grams, 2,195 yards)
Crochet hook, size I (5.50 mm) **or** size needed
for gauge
1/2"w Ribbon - 14 yards
Sewing needle and thread

GAUGE: In pattern, (dc, ch 1) 6 times = 3¹/₂";
4 rows = 3"

Gauge Swatch: 4¹/₄"w x 3"h
Ch 18 **loosely.**
Work same as Afghan Body for 4 rows.
Finish off.

AFGHAN BODY
Ch 148 **loosely.**

Row 1 (Right side)**:** Dc in sixth ch from hook, ★ ch 1,
skip next ch, dc in next ch; repeat from ★ across: 72 sps.

Note: Loop a short piece of yarn around any stitch to
mark Row 1 as **right** side.

Row 2: Ch 4 **(counts as first dc plus ch 1, now
and throughout)**, turn; (dc in next dc, ch 1) across to
last sp, skip next ch, dc in next ch: 73 dc.

Rows 3-6: Ch 4, turn; dc in next dc, (ch 1, dc in next
dc) across.

Row 7: Ch 4, turn; (dc in next dc, ch 1) 5 times, 3 dc in
next dc, (skip next 2 dc, 6 dc in next dc) 19 times, skip
next 2 dc, 3 dc in next dc, (ch 1, dc in next dc) 6 times:
19 6-dc groups.

Rows 8-78: Ch 4, turn; (dc in next dc, ch 1) 5 times,
3 dc in next dc, 6 dc in sp **between** center dc of each
6-dc group across to next 3-dc group, skip next 2 dc,
3 dc in next dc, (ch 1, dc in next dc) 6 times.

Row 79: Ch 4, turn; (dc in next dc, ch 1) 7 times,
★ skip next dc, dc in next dc, ch 1; repeat from ★ across
to next ch-1 sp, dc in next dc, (ch 1, dc in next dc) 5
times: 72 ch-1 sps.

Rows 80-84: Ch 4, turn; dc in next dc, (ch 1, dc in
next dc) across; do **not** finish off.

EDGING
TOP - FIRST SCALLOP
Row 1: Turn; slip st in first dc, (slip st in next ch-1 sp
and in next dc) 4 times, ch 7, skip next 4 sps, slip st in
next st, slip st in next sp and in next st, leave remaining
sts unworked.

Row 2: Turn; 14 dc in ch-7 sp, skip next sp, slip st in
next st and in next sp, slip st in next st: 14 dc.

Row 3: Ch 1, turn; (dc in next dc, ch 1) 14 times, skip
next sp, slip st in next st, slip st in next sp and in next st.

Row 4: Ch 4, turn; (sc in next ch-1 sp, ch 4) 15 times,
skip next sp, slip st in next st, slip st in next sp and in
next st.

Row 5: Ch 4, turn; (sc in next ch-4 sp, ch 4) 16 times,
skip next sp, slip st in next st; do **not** finish off.

TOP - NEXT 5 SCALLOPS
Row 1: (Slip st in next sp and in next st) 4 times, ch 7,
skip next 4 sps, slip st in next st, slip st in next sp and in
next st, leave remaining sts unworked.

Rows 2-5: Work same as Top - First Scallop.

SIDE - FIRST SCALLOP
Row 1: Working across end of rows, slip st in first sp
and in next st (top of dc), (slip st in next sp and in next st)
3 times, ch 7, skip next 4 sps, slip st in next st, slip st in
next sp and in next st, leave remaining sts unworked.

Rows 2-5: Work same as Top - First Scallop.

SIDE - NEXT 6 SCALLOPS
Rows 1-5: Work same as Top - Next 5 Scallops.

BOTTOM - FIRST SCALLOP
Row 1: Working in free loops of beginning ch and in
ch-1 sps *(Fig. 3b, page 1)*, (slip st in next sp and in next
st) 4 times, ch 7, skip next 4 sps, slip st in next st, slip st
in next sp and in next st, leave remaining sts unworked.

Rows 2-5: Work same as Top - First Scallop.

BOTTOM - NEXT 5 SCALLOPS
Rows 1-5: Work same as Top - Next 5 Scallops.

SECOND SIDE
Work same as first Side.

Finish off.

FINISHING
Using photo as a guide for placement, page 35, weave
ribbon through sps along outer sps of Afghan Body; sew
ends together.

Leaving 4 sps free between outer ribbon and inner
ribbon, weave ribbon through sps along inner sps of
Afghan Body leaving a 10" length at each corner. Repeat
for remaining 3 sides.

Tie ends in a bow at each corner.

Design by Maggie Weldon.

Winter Warmers

Finished Size: 44½" x 63½"

MATERIALS

Worsted Weight Yarn:
Solid version
Ecru - 57 ounces, (1,620 grams, 3,585 yards)
Striped version
Green - 24 ounces, (680 grams, 1,510 yards)
Ecru - 19 ounces, (540 grams, 1,195 yards)
Rose - 14 ounces, (400 grams, 880 yards)
Crochet hook, size H (5.00 mm) **or** size needed
for gauge

GAUGE: In pattern, 14 sts = 4";
14 rows (one repeat) = 6"

Gauge Swatch: 5"w x 6"h
Ch 19 **loosely**.
Work same as Afghan Body for 14 rows: 17 sc.
Finish off.

STITCH GUIDE

FRONT POST DOUBLE CROCHET
(abbreviated FPdc)
YO, insert hook from **front** to **back** around post of
dc indicated *(Fig. 4, page 2)*, YO and pull up a loop
(3 loops on hook), (YO and draw through 2 loops on
hook) twice.

BACK POST DOUBLE CROCHET
(abbreviated BPdc)
YO, insert hook from **back** to **front** around post of
dc indicated *(Fig. 4, page 2)*, YO and pull up a loop
(3 loops on hook), (YO and draw through 2 loops on
hook) twice.

FRONT POST CLUSTER
(abbreviated FP Cluster)
YO, skip next st, insert hook from **front** to **back**
around post of next dc *(Fig. 4, page 2)*, YO and pull
up a loop, YO and draw through 2 loops on hook,
YO twice, insert hook from **front** to **back** around
post of next dc, YO and pull up a loop, (YO and draw
through 2 loops on hook) twice, YO 3 times, insert
hook from **front** to **back** around post of next dc, YO
and pull up a loop, (YO and draw through
2 loops on hook) 3 times, YO and draw through all
4 loops on hook.

BACK POST CLUSTER
(abbreviated BP Cluster)
YO, skip next st, insert hook from **back** to **front**
around post of next dc *(Fig. 4, page 2)*, YO and pull
up a loop, YO and draw through 2 loops on hook,
YO twice, insert hook from **back** to **front** around
post of next dc, YO and pull up a loop, (YO and draw
through 2 loops on hook) twice, YO 3 times, insert
hook from **back** to **front** around post of next dc, YO
and pull up a loop, (YO and draw through
2 loops on hook) 3 times, YO and draw through all
4 loops on hook.

Note: Each row is worked across length of Afghan. For
Solid Version, do **not** change colors.

AFGHAN BODY

With Ecru, ch 223 **loosely**.

Row 1 (Right side)**:** Dc in fourth ch from hook and in
each ch across changing to Green in last dc *(Fig. 2a,
page 1)*: 221 sts.

Row 2: Ch 3 **(counts as first dc, now and
throughout)**, turn; dc in next dc, ★ work BP Cluster,
working in **front** of BP Cluster, dc in same 3 dc;
repeat from ★ across to last 3 sts, dc in last 3 sts:
54 BP Clusters.

Row 3: Ch 3, turn; dc in next dc, ★ work FP Cluster,
working **behind** FP Cluster, dc in same 3 dc; repeat
from ★ across to last 3 sts, dc in last 3 sts changing to
Ecru in last dc.

Row 4: Ch 3, turn; dc in next dc and in each st across
changing to Rose in last dc: 221 dc.

Row 5: Ch 3, turn; dc in next dc and in each dc across:
221 dc.

Row 6: Ch 3, turn; work FPdc around next dc, (work
BPdc around next dc, work FPdc around next dc) across
to last dc, dc in last dc changing to Ecru.

Row 7: Ch 1, turn; sc in each st across: 221 sc.

Row 8: Ch 3, turn; dc in next sc and in each sc across
changing to Green in last dc.

Row 9: Ch 3, turn; dc in next dc, ★ work FP
Cluster, working **behind** FP Cluster, dc in same 3
dc; repeat from ★ across to last 3 sts, dc in last 3 dc:
54 FP Clusters.

Row 10: Ch 3, turn; dc in next dc, ★ work BP Cluster,
working in **front** of BP Cluster, dc in same 3 dc; repeat
from ★ across to last 3 sts, dc in last 3 sts changing to
Ecru in last dc.

Rows 11-15: Repeat Rows 4-8.

Rows 16-101: Repeat Rows 2-15, 6 times; then
repeat Rows 2 and 3 once **more**.

Row 102: Ch 3, turn; dc in next dc and in each st
across; do **not** finish off.

Continued on page 53.

EDGING

Ch 1, turn; sc evenly around entire Afghan Body working 3 sc in each corner; join with slip st to first sc, finish off.

Using photo as a guide for placement, page 34, and holding 4 strands of corresponding color yarn together, each 12" long, add fringe evenly spaced across end of rows (Figs. 6c & d, page 2).

Design by Nair Carswell.

Finished Size: 46½" x 64"

MATERIALS

Worsted Weight Yarn:
Black - 33 ounces, (940 grams, 2,075 yards)
Natural - 15 ounces, (430 grams, 945 yards)
Grey - 12 ounces, (340 grams, 755 yards)
Crochet hook, size I (5.50 mm) **or** size needed for gauge

GAUGE: 15 sc and 15 rows = 4"

Gauge Swatch: 5½"w x 4"h
With Black, ch 21 **loosely**.
Work same as Afghan Body through Row 15.
Finish off.

AFGHAN BODY

With Black, ch 174 **loosely**.

Row 1 (Right side): Sc in second ch from hook and in each ch across: 173 sc.

Note: Loop a short piece of yarn around any stitch to mark Row 1 as **right** side.

Row 2: Ch 1, turn; sc in each sc across.

Note: When changing colors (Fig. 2a, page 1), work **over** unused color, holding it with normal tension and keeping yarn to **wrong** side; do **not** cut yarn until color is no longer needed.

Rows 3-238: Repeat Row 2 for pattern, following Rows 3-28 of Chart once, then follow Rows 1-28 of Chart, 7 times; then follow Rows 1-14 of Chart once **more**; do **not** finish off.

EDGING

Rnd 1: Ch 1, turn; 3 sc in first sc, work 170 sc evenly spaced across to last sc, 3 sc in last sc; sc in end of each row across; working in free loops of beginning ch (Fig. 3b, page 1), 3 sc in first ch, work 170 sc evenly spaced across to ch at base of last sc, 3 sc in ch at base of last sc; sc in end of each row across; join with slip st to first sc: 828 sc.

Rnd 2: Ch 1, do **not** turn; sc in same st and in each sc around working 3 sc in center sc of each corner 3-sc group; join with slip st to first sc: 836 sc.

Rnd 3: Ch 1, sc in same st and in next sc, (sc, ch 2, sc) in next sc, † ch 2, skip next 2 sc, ★ sc in next 2 sc, ch 2, skip next 2 sc; repeat from ★ across to center sc of next corner 3-sc group, (sc, ch 2, sc) in center sc †, sc in each sc across to center sc of next corner 3-sc group, (sc, ch 2, sc) in center sc, repeat from † to † once, sc in each sc across; join with slip st to first sc, finish off.

Holding 10 strands of Black yarn together, each 16" long, add fringe in each ch-2 sp across short edges of Afghan (Figs. 6a & b, page 2).

Design by Melissa Leapman.

CHART

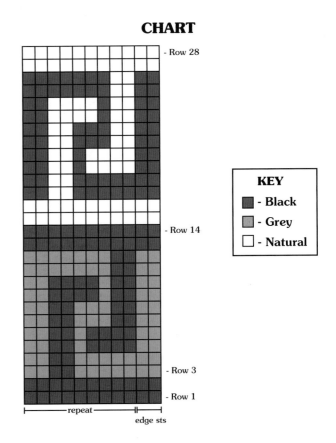

KEY
- Black
- Grey
- Natural

On **right** side rows, follow Chart from **right** to **left**, working 2 edge sts, then working repeat across.

On **wrong** side rows, follow Chart from **left** to **right**, working repeat across to last 2 sts, then working 2 edge sts.

Young at Heart

Finished Size: 43" x 71"

MATERIALS
Worsted Weight Yarn:
Off-White - 58 ounces,
    (1,650 grams, 3,810 yards)
Blue - 2½ ounces, (70 grams, 165 yards)
Green - 2½ ounces, (70 grams, 165 yards)
Rose - 2 ounces, (60 grams, 130 yards)
Crochet hooks, sizes I (5.50 mm) **and** J (6.00 mm) **or**
    sizes needed for gauge
Yarn needle

GAUGE: With large size hook, 13 sc and 14 rows = 4"
    With small size hook, 14 dc = 4"

Gauge Swatch: 4" square
With large size hook, ch 14 **loosely**.
Row 1: Sc in second ch from hook and in each ch
across: 13 sc.
Rows 2-14: Ch 1, turn; sc in each sc across.
Finish off.

CENTER PANEL
With Off-White and large size hook, ch 32 **loosely**.

Row 1 (Right side)**:** Sc in second ch from hook and in
each ch across: 31 sc.

Note: Loop a short piece of yarn around any stitch to
mark Row 1 as **right** side and bottom edge.

Rows 2-8: Ch 1, turn; sc in each sc across.

*Note: When changing colors (Fig. 2a, page 1), keep
unused color on* **wrong** *side of work; do* **not** *cut yarn
until color is no longer needed. Use a separate skein or
ball for each color change.*

Row 9: Ch 1, turn; sc in first 15 sc changing to Blue in
last sc made, sc in next sc changing to Off-White, sc in
each sc across.

Rows 10-22: Follow Chart A.

Row 23: Ch 1, turn; sc in first 10 sc changing to Blue
in last sc made, cut Off-White, sc in next 3 sc changing
to Off-White in last sc made, cut Blue, sc in next 5 sc
changing to Blue in last sc made, cut Off-White, sc in
next 3 sc changing to Off-White in last sc made, cut Blue,
sc in each sc across.

Rows 24-78: Ch 1, turn; sc in each sc across.

Rows 79-233: Repeat Rows 9-78 twice, then repeat
Rows 9-23 once **more**.

Rows 234-241: Ch 1, turn; sc in each sc across; do
not finish off.

CHART A

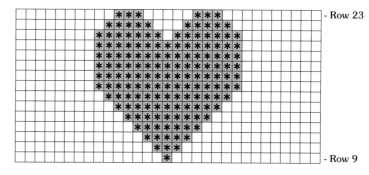

- Row 23

- Row 9

KEY
☐ - Off-White sc
✱ - Blue sc

TRIM
FIRST SIDE
Change to small size hook.

Row 1: Ch 4 **(counts as first dc plus ch 1, now
and throughout)**, do **not** turn; working in end of rows,
skip first 2 rows, dc in next row, ★ ch 1, skip next row,
dc in next row; repeat from ★ across: 121 dc.

Row 2: Ch 3 **(counts as first dc, now and
throughout)**, turn; dc in next ch-1 sp and in each dc
and each ch-1 sp across: 241 dc.

Row 3: Ch 3, turn; dc in next dc and in each dc across.

Row 4: Ch 1, turn; sc in each dc across.

Rows 5 and 6: Ch 3, turn; dc in next st and in each st
across.

Row 7: Ch 4, turn; skip next dc, dc in next dc, ★
ch 1, skip next dc, dc in next dc; repeat from ★ across;
finish off: 121 dc.

SECOND SIDE
Row 1: Hold Panel with **right** side facing and bottom
edge to your **right**; with small size hook and working in
end of rows, join Off-White with slip st in first row; ch 4,
skip next row, dc in next row, ★ ch 1, skip next row, dc
in next row; repeat from ★ across: 121 dc.

Rows 2-7: Work same as First Side.

LEFT PANEL
Work same as Center Panel through Row 6 of Trim
First Side: 241 dc.

Finish off.

RIGHT PANEL
Work same as Center Panel through Row 241.

Finish off.

TRIM
Work same as Second Side through Row 6: 241 dc.

Finish off.

54

Continued on page 55.

FINISHING

With Green, add cross stitch design to each Panel between hearts following Chart B, page 56, **and** to each Panel Trim across Row 4 (sc row) following Chart C, page 56, as follows:

Each square on the Chart represents one sc and each shaded square represents one cross stitch worked over a sc. Thread a yarn needle with a long strand of color indicated. With **right** side facing and holding bottom edge toward you, bring needle up at 1 leaving a 3" end on back. Work over this end to secure. Insert needle down at 2 (half Cross made), bring needle up at 3 and go down at 4 **(Cross Stitch completed, *Fig. 19*)**.

Fig. 19

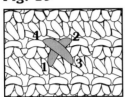

With Green, add Satin St leaves to each Panel Trim following Chart C.

With Rose, add Satin St flowers to each Panel following Chart B, **and** add Satin St buds to each Panel Trim following Chart C as follows:

Work a series of straight stitches by entering and exiting the same hole. Bring needle up at 1 and go down at 2 *(Fig. 20)*.

Fig. 20

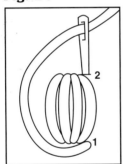

With Rose, add French Knot flower centers to each Panel as follows:

Bring needle up at 1, wrap yarn desired number of times around needle and go down at 2, holding end of yarn with non-stitching fingers *(Fig. 21)*. Tighten knot; then pull needle through, holding yarn until it must be released.

Fig. 21

ASSEMBLY

With Off-White, working through **both** loops, and holding bottom edges at same end, whipstitch Panels together beginning in first st and ending in last st *(Fig. 5a, page 2)*.

EDGING

Rnd 1: With **right** side facing and small size hook, join Off-White with slip st in end of first row at top right corner; ch 3, dc in same row, ch 1, (dc in end of next row, ch 1) 5 times, † dc in first st of next Panel, ch 1, (skip next st, dc in next st, ch 1) 15 times, **[**(dc in end of next row, ch 1) 7 times, dc in first st of next Panel, ch 1, (skip next st, dc in next st, ch 1) 15 times**]** twice, (dc in end of next row, ch 1) 5 times, (2 dc, ch 2, 2 dc) in end of last row, ch 1; working across long edge, ★ skip next dc, dc in next dc, ch 1; repeat from ★ across to last 2 dc, skip last 2 dc †; working across bottom edge, (2 dc, ch 2, 2 dc) in first row, ch 1, (dc in end of next row, ch 1) 5 times, working in free loops of beginning ch *(Fig. 3b, page 1)*, repeat from † to † once, 2 dc in same sp as first dc, ch 2; join with slip st to first dc.

Rnd 2: Ch 1, sc in first 2 dc, 2 sc in each ch-1 sp across to within 2 dc of corner ch-2 sp, sc in next 2 dc, (2 sc, ch 1, 2 sc) in corner ch-2 sp, ★ sc in next 2 dc, 2 sc in each ch-1 sp across to within 2 dc of corner ch-2 sp, sc in next 2 dc, (2 sc, ch 1, 2 sc) in corner ch-2 sp; repeat from ★ 2 times **more**; join with slip st to first sc, finish off.

Holding 4 strands of Off-White yarn together, each 13" long, add fringe evenly spaced across short edges of Afghan *(Figs. 6a & b, page 2)*.

Design by Sheila Hardy.

CHART B

- Row 79
- Row 70
- Row 60
- Row 50
- Row 40
- Row 30
- Row 23
- Row 20

CHART C

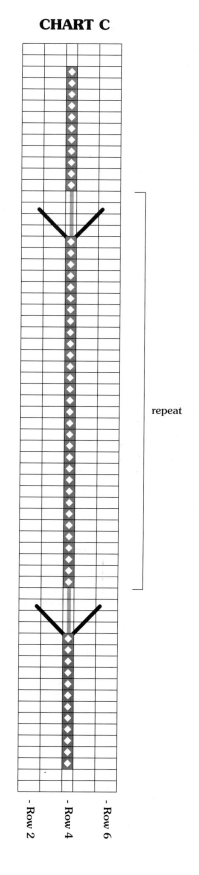

repeat

- Row 2
- Row 4
- Row 6

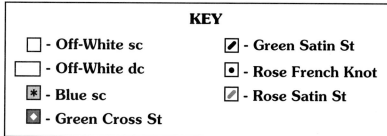

KEY

☐ - Off-White sc

▭ - Off-White dc

✳ - Blue sc

◈ - Green Cross St

◢ - Green Satin St

⊙ - Rose French Knot

╱ - Rose Satin St

56

Zest for the West

Finished Size: 49" x 64"

MATERIALS
Worsted Weight Yarn:
    Red - 35 ounces, (990 grams, 2,300 yards)
    White - 11 ounces, (310 grams, 725 yards)
    Black - 5 ounces, (140 grams, 330 yards)
Crochet hook, size I (5.50 mm) **or** size needed
    for gauge
Yarn needle

GAUGE: Each Square = $7^1/_2$"

Gauge Swatch: $3^3/_4$" square
Work same as Square through Rnd 5.

STITCH GUIDE

> **TREBLE CROCHET (abbreviated tr)**
> YO twice, insert hook in st or sp indicated, YO and
> pull up a loop (4 loops on hook), (YO and draw
> through 2 loops on hook) 3 times.

SQUARE (Make 48)
Rnd 1 (Right side)**:** With White, ch 5, (dc, ch 1) 7 times
in fifth ch from hook; join with slip st to fourth ch of
beginning ch-5, finish off: 8 ch-1 sps.

Note: Loop a short piece of yarn around any stitch to
mark Rnd 1 as **right** side.

Rnd 2: With **right** side facing, join Red with slip st
in any ch-1 sp; ch 3 **(counts as first dc, now and
throughout)**, 2 dc in same sp, (dc, ch 1, tr, ch 1, dc) in
next ch-1 sp, ★ 3 dc in next ch-1 sp, (dc, ch 1, tr, ch 1,
dc) in next ch-1 sp; repeat from ★ 2 times **more**; join
with slip st to first dc, finish off: 24 sts and 8 ch-1 sps.

Rnd 3: With **wrong** side facing, join Black with sc in
ch to **right** of any corner tr *(see Joining With Sc,
page 1)*; ch 3, ★ skip next corner tr, sc in next ch,
working in dc and in chs, (ch 1, skip next dc, sc in next
st) 3 times, ch 3; repeat from ★ 2 times **more**, skip next
corner tr, (sc in next st, ch 1, skip next dc) 3 times; join
with slip st to first sc, finish off: 16 sps.

Rnd 4: With **right** side facing, join Red with sc in sc
to **right** of any corner ch-3 sp; ★ † working in **front** of
next ch-3, (dc, ch 1, tr, ch 1, dc) in corner tr one rnd
below ch-3, (sc in next sc, working **behind** next ch-1,
dc in skipped dc one rnd **below** ch-1) 3 times †, sc in
next sc; repeat from ★ 2 times **more**, then repeat from
† to † once; join with slip st to first sc, do **not** finish off:
40 sts and 8 ch-1 sps.

Rnd 5: Ch 1, sc in same st and in next 2 sts, ch 3,
★ skip next corner tr, sc in next 11 sts, ch 3; repeat from
★ 2 times **more**, skip next corner tr, sc in last 8 sts; join
with slip st to first sc, finish off: 44 sc and 4 ch-3 sps.

Rnd 6: With **wrong** side facing, join White with slip st
in sc to **right** of any corner ch-3 sp; ch 3, 5 dc in corner
ch-3 sp, dc in next sc, ★ (ch 1, skip next sc, dc in next sc)
5 times, 5 dc in next corner ch-3 sp, dc in next sc; repeat
from ★ 2 times **more**, ch 1, skip next sc, (dc in next
sc, ch 1, skip next sc) across; join with slip st to first dc,
finish off: 20 ch-1 sps.

Rnd 7: With **right** side facing, join Red with sc in
dc to **right** of first dc of any corner 5-dc group; sc in
next 2 dc, ★ † (dc, ch 2, dc) in next dc, sc in next 3 dc,
working in **front** of next ch-1, tr in skipped sc one rnd
below ch-1, sc in next dc, (working **behind** next ch-1, tr
in skipped sc one rnd **below** ch-1, sc in next dc) 3 times,
working in **front** of next ch-1, tr in skipped sc one rnd
below ch-1 †, sc in next 3 dc; repeat from ★ 2 times
more, then repeat from † to † once; join with slip st to
first sc, finish off: 68 sts and 4 ch-2 sps.

Rnd 8: With **wrong** side facing, join Black with sc in
dc to **right** of any corner ch-2 sp; ch 3, skip next corner
ch-2 sp, sc in next dc, ★ (ch 1, skip next sc, sc in next
st) 8 times, ch 3, skip next corner ch-2 sp, sc in next dc;
repeat from ★ 2 times **more**, ch 1, skip next sc, (sc in
next st, ch 1, skip next sc) across; join with slip st to first
sc, finish off: 36 sc and 36 sps.

Rnd 9: With **right** side facing, join Red with sc in sc to
right of any corner ch-3 sp; ★ † working **behind** next
ch-3, (dc, ch 1, tr, ch 1, dc) in corner ch-2 sp one rnd
below ch-3, (sc in next sc, working **behind** next ch-1,
dc in skipped sc one rnd **below** ch-1) twice, (sc in next
sc, working in **front** of next ch-1, dc in skipped sc one
rnd **below** ch-1) 4 times, (sc in next sc, working **behind**
next ch-1, dc in skipped sc one rnd **below** ch-1) twice †,
sc in next sc; repeat from ★ 2 times **more**, then repeat
from † to † once; join with slip st to first sc, finish off:
80 sts and 8 ch-1 sps.